CHOLA

Sacred Bronzes of Southern India

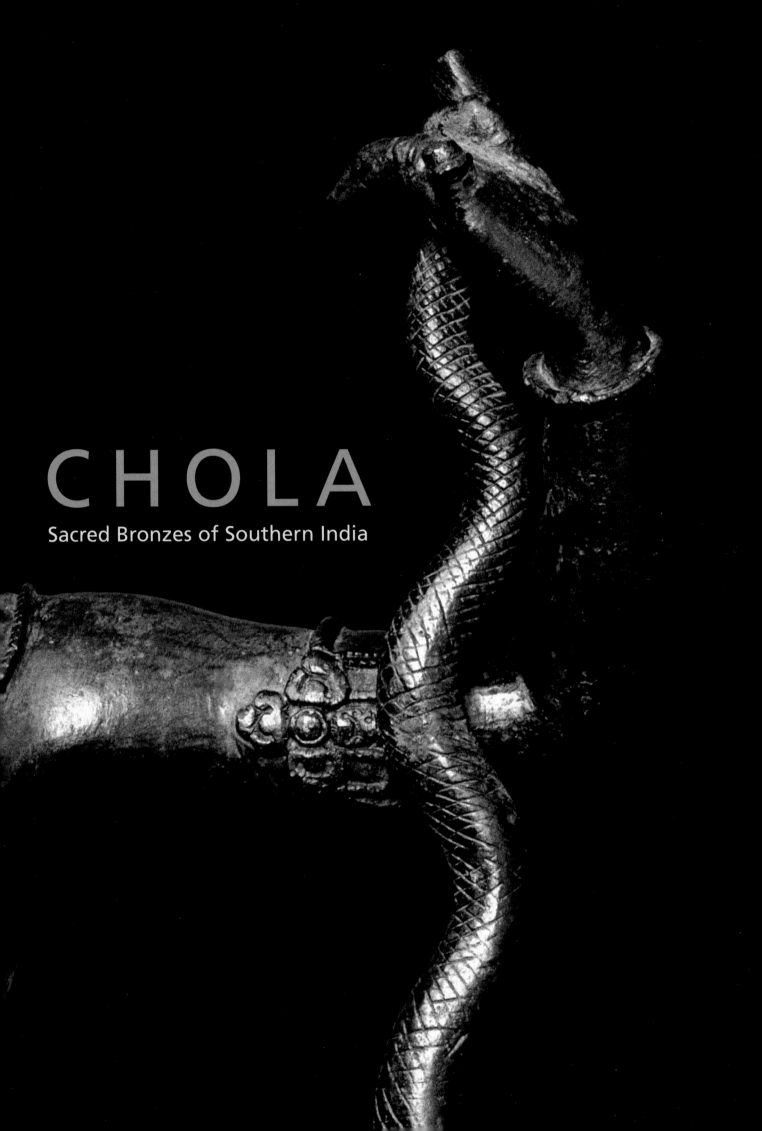

CHOLA

Sacred Bronzes of Southern India

First published on the occasion of the exhibition
'Chola: Sacred Bronzes of Southern India'

Royal Academy of Arts, London
11 November 2006 – 25 February 2007

Travel Partner

The Royal Academy of Arts is grateful
to Her Majesty's Government for agreeing
to indemnify this exhibition under the
National Heritage Act 1980, and to Resource,
The Council for Museums, Archives and Libraries,
for its help in arranging the indemnity.

EXHIBITION CURATORS
Vidya Dehejia
John Eskenazi
Adrian Locke
Norman Rosenthal

EXHIBITION ORGANISATION
Lucy Hunt

PHOTOGRAPHIC AND COPYRIGHT CO-ORDINATION
Miranda Bennion

CATALOGUE
Royal Academy Publications
David Breuer
Harry Burden
Claire Callow
Carola Krueger
Peter Sawbridge
Nick Tite

TRANSLATION FROM THE FRENCH (AUGUSTE RODIN):
Caroline Beamish
COPY-EDITING AND PROOFREADING: Philippa Baker
BOOK DESIGN, LAYOUT AND CARTOGRAPHY:
Isambard Thomas, London
PICTURE RESEARCH: Sara Ayad
COLOUR ORIGINATION: DawkinsColour
Printed in Belgium by Die Keure

British Library Cataloguing-in-Publication Data
A catalogue record for this book is available
from the British Library

HARDBACK
ISBN 10: 1-903973-83-X
ISBN 13: 978-1-903973-83-7

SOFTBACK
ISBN 10: 1-903973-84-8
ISBN 13: 978-1-903973-84-4

Distributed outside the United States and Canada
by Thames & Hudson Ltd, London

Distributed in the United States and Canada
by Harry N. Abrams, Inc., New York

EDITORIAL NOTE
Measurements are given in centimetres,
height before width.

Pages 2–3: detail of cat. 25
Page 7: detail of cat. 4
Pages 8–9: detail of cat. 6

ACKNOWLEDGEMENTS
The curators are most grateful
to the following individuals,
without whose assistance this
exhibition would not have
been possible:

R. Balasubramanian
Melissa Chiu
Willard Clark
Stanislaw Czuma
J. E. Dawson
Vishakha Desai
Nancy Grossman
John Guy
Jennifer Howes
Lesley Jacob
R. Kannan
Subhash Kapoor
Christine Knoke
Robert Knox
Steven Kossak
Gerd Kreisel
Sanjib Kumar Singh
Amy McEwan
Stephen A. Markel
Darielle Mason
Simon Ray
M. A. Siddique
Raghuraj Singh Chauhan
Pavan K. Varma
S. Venkataraman
C. Vijayara Kumar
Clair Whiteman
Doris Wiener
Marianne Yaldiz

President's Foreword

Nearly sixty years ago, on 14 August 1947, the Republic of India secured independence from British rule. Later that same year the Royal Academy hosted an 'Exhibition of Art Chiefly from the Dominions of India and Pakistan'. Within this extraordinary assembly of nearly 1,500 objects, ranging in date from 2400 BCE to the present day, a gallery was given over to a display of south Indian bronzes from the ninth to the eighteenth centuries. Two Chola representations of Shiva Nataraja (Lord of Dance) from the Government Museum in Madras (modern-day Chennai) were shown against a backdrop of printed temple hangings from the Victoria and Albert Museum. These were the same two bronzes that the sculptor Auguste Rodin had written about so passionately in Paris in 1913; his text has been newly translated for this catalogue.

As India prepares to celebrate sixty years of independence, the Royal Academy is delighted to host an exhibition of Indian art once again. To do justice to this vast country, with its extraordinary wealth of history and art, the Royal Academy will be presenting India in a series of small, culturally specific exhibitions. The first of these, 'Chola: Sacred Bronzes of Southern India', features a selection of cast-bronze sculptures from the region in the far south known as Tamil Nadu. They date from the period 850 to 1250, when the territory was under the rule of the imperial Chola dynasty. Many such works continue to be worshipped in the temples for which they were originally commissioned, in some cases over a thousand years ago.

We would like to thank all our lenders, especially the National Museum of India in New Delhi, the Government Museum in Chennai, the Cleveland Museum of Art and the Asia Society in New York, for lending so generously to this exhibition. We would also like to thank our two curators, Professor Vidya Dehejia, Barbara Stoler Miller Professor of Indian and South Asian Art at Columbia University, New York, and John Eskenazi, for their knowledge and expertise. They have been ably supported by Norman Rosenthal and Adrian Locke. The exhibition designer Calum Storrie also deserves our gratitude.

Naturally, no exhibition of this kind would be possible without the generous support of many individuals. We would like to take this opportunity to thank Her Excellency Ms Ambika Soni, Minister of Tourism and Culture, Government of India, His Excellency Mr Kamalesh Sharma, High Commissioner of India, London, Mr Badal K. Das, Secretary, Department of Culture, Ministry of Culture and Tourism, Dr Atul Khare, Director, The Nehru Centre, London, and Dr A. K. V. S. Reddy, Director-General, National Museum and Vice Chancellor, National Museum Institute, New Delhi. All have been enormously supportive of the exhibition and have given us great assistance in facilitating the Indian loans.

Sir Nicholas Grimshaw CBE
President, Royal Academy of Arts

Map
The Chola territories
in southern India,
c. 850–1250

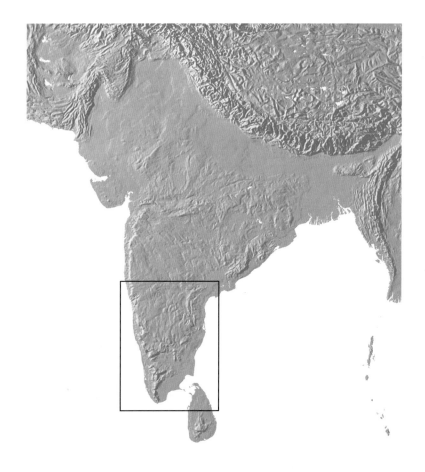

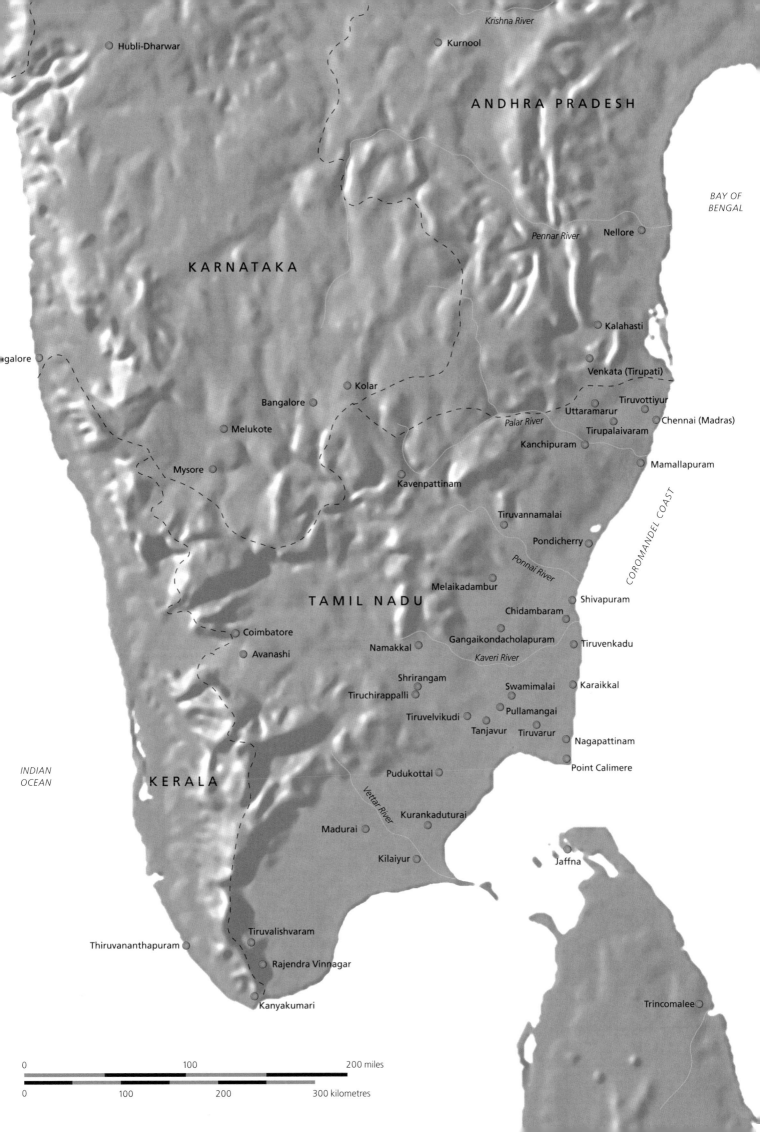

Hubli-Dharwar

Kurnool

Krishna River

ANDHRA PRADESH

BAY OF
BENGAL

Pennar River

Nellore

KARNATAKA

Kalahasti

galore

Venkata (Tirupati)

Kolar

Tiruvottiyur

Bangalore

Uttaramarur

Palar River

Tirupalaivaram

Chennai (Madras)

Melukote

Kanchipuram

Mysore

Mamallapuram

Kavenpattinam

Tiruvannamalai

Pondicherry

Ponnai River

COROMANDEL COAST

Melaikadambur

Shivapuram

TAMIL NADU

Chidambaram

Gangaikondacholapuram

Tiruvenkadu

Coimbatore

Namakkal

Kaveri River

Avanashi

Shrirangam

Karaikkal

Swamimalai

Tiruchirappalli

Pullamangai

Tiruvelvikudi

Tanjavur

Tiruvarur

Nagapattinam

INDIAN
OCEAN

Pudukottal

Point Calimere

KERALA

Vettar River

Kurankaduturai

Madurai

Kilaiyur

Jaffna

Tiruvalishvaram

Thiruvananthapuram

Rajendra Vinnagar

Kanyakumari

Trincomalee

| 0 | | 100 | | 200 miles |
| 0 | 100 | 200 | | 300 kilometres |

I Parading the Gods: Bronze Devotional Images of Chola South India

JOHN GUY

WORSHIP BEYOND THE TEMPLE

IN SOUTH INDIA portable icons of the gods came into existence for a very particular purpose: to allow the parading of the deity away from the temple sanctuary for both the god's pleasure and the spiritual benefit of devotees. In a practice that continues to the present day, the god ventures forth both to see and to be seen – *darshan*.[1] The small-scale metal sculptures – *utsavamurti* – are empowered through special rites to act on behalf of immovable images installed in the temple. Some are employed on a daily basis for ceremonies in which they are processed within the temple compound, pausing at intervals to allow offerings. In weekly and monthly festivals the icons are paraded to altars and pillared halls (*mandapas*) within the temple compound to receive offerings or to be bathed and adorned. For the gods to venture outside their temple compound is a special event, usually confined to annual festival processions. The climax of such a parade is the immersion of the icon in a river or its temporary installation in a forest grove (fig. 2). Both rites serve to link the prosperity of the land to the god's grace and invite the god's benevolence.

The artistic production of cast-metal icons of the gods was directly linked to the emergence of new devotional and ritual practices in India in the early centuries of the first millennium CE. A wave of devotional Hinduism (*bhakti*) swept across south India from the sixth to the tenth centuries, finding its voice in the poetry written by a number of wandering mendicants – visionaries who dedicated their lives to composing and reciting hymns and verse in praise of their chosen god. These inspired and inspirational figures were 'canonised' as poet-saints – sixty-three Shaiva *nayanmar* (spiritual guides or leaders, followers of Shiva) and twelve Vaishnava *alvar* ('immersed in god', followers of Vishnu).

Along with these theological developments came a move to design and build large structural temples to house the permanent cult images and provide focal points for devotees. The Pallava period (*c.*600–850/900) was marked by a rapid expansion in temple building in south India. The finest temples, built under royal patronage, are the Kailashnatha (early eighth century) and Vaikuntaperumal (*c.*775) temples in Kanchipuram, and the Shore Temple at Mamallapuram, located at the Pallava kingdom's capital city and major port respectively. These temples, with their deep porches, dark interiors and constricting enclosure walls, mark the transition from cave shrines and rock-cut temples to the beginnings of the mature free-standing south Indian or Dravidian-style temple.

The relentless drive to build new and grander temples – a process very much intertwined with the political and social dynamics of the age[2] – and the arrival of the singing *bhaktas* gave enormous strength to

Fig. 1
Thomas Daniell, *The Great Bull: a Hindoo Idol at Tanjore*, 1792. Aquatint, published in Thomas and William Daniell, *Oriental Scenery: Twenty-four Views in Hindoostan*, London, 1797

a revivalist Hinduism, which was winning a long struggle against Buddhism and Jainism for the hearts and souls of the populace. The poet-saints travelled widely in south India, from one temple and holy site (*tirtha*) to another, propagating and proselytising. It is said that the four most famous Shaiva poet-saints – Appar, Sambandar, Sundarar and Manikkavachakar – between them visited 274 temples and referred to many others in their hymns.[3] At each temple or holy place the saints composed a hymn, written in Tamil, in praise of their god, celebrating the place as one associated with the grace of Shiva or Vishnu and so defining it as a *patal perra talam* – 'a place sung by the saints'. In this way the poet-saints made the Tamil landscape a sacred landscape of living Hinduism, claiming wherever they sang their songs of praise as the land of Shiva or Vishnu.

Tamil Nadu, where the poet-saints were most active, became their spiritual battleground. More than half of the temples named ('sung') by these saints were in Tanjavur district, the Pallava and Chola heartland along the Kaveri River and its delta. The Hindu saints claimed many victories over exponents of Jainism and Buddhism – the 'secular faiths'. Indeed Appar was a convert from Jainism and, with all the vigour of the newly converted, preached fervently against his former faith, even succeeding in converting the Pallava king of Kanchipuram, Mahendravarman I (r. c. 610–30) to the worship of Shiva.[4]

THE CHOLAS

For most of the second half of the first millennium, south India was ruled by the Pallavas, based at Kanchipuram, the Pandyas to the south, centred at Madurai, and the Cheras to the west. In the ninth century the Cholas emerged as a lesser vassal state, controlling Tanjavur but paying allegiance to Pallava suzerainty. In about 850 they began to assert their independence, securing Tanjavur and claiming this city henceforth as their capital. Under Aditya Chola (r. 871–907), a gifted general and diplomat and the effective founder of the Chola Empire, within twenty-five years the Cholas consolidated a formidable power base in the Tanjavur and Kaveri area. They also made significant conquests in Tondai Nadu, seizing territory from the Pallava and Pandya kingdoms and from the Gangas to the north,

Fig. 2
An icon of Shiva as Vrishabhavana is washed with the waters of the Kaveri River, Swetaranyeswarar temple, Tanjavur. Photograph by the author, April 1993

Fig. 3
Bejewelled and garlanded Shiva being paraded, Panguni Uttiram festival, Kapalishvara temple, Mylapur, Chennai. Photograph by the author, March 2003

aided by the Cheras, with whom they formed strategic alliances. At the beginning of Parantaka I's reign (r. 907–55), Chola territory extended north to Chennai (Madras) as far as Kalahasti on the Andhra Pradesh borders (see map, p. 10). In the course of his long reign the Pallavas were subjugated and subsumed into the Chola state, as was the ancient Pandya royal household of Madurai.

Once the Chola-mandalam[5] – the territory of the Cholas – was established, Parantaka and his successors quickly sought to affirm their right to rule through public acts of benefaction. The building of massive temples generously equipped with devotional images and endowed with funds to ensure that sacred rites were performed in perpetuity became their foremost objective in the public arena. Rajaraja Chola (r. 985–1014) closely supervised the construction of the largest temple built in the Indian subcontinent up to that date, the Rajarajeshvara at Tanjavur (fig. 1). Rajendra Chola (r. 1012–44) emulated his father's example in the building of a mighty temple at Gangaikondacholapuram, his short-lived new capital city. All these temples had to be equipped with both fixed and portable images of devotion.

A description of the parade of a processional bronze of Shiva as Nataraja (Lord of Dance) at Chidambaram is of special importance in this context. Nataraja, enshrined at his home in the golden hall at Chidambaram, had assumed the status of tutelary deity (kula-nayakam) to the Chola royal household. This association may have been established as early as the reign of Parantaka I, who, as a devout follower of Shiva, first undertook the gilding of Shiva Nataraja's dwelling, the chit sabha, and thereafter acquired the title of 'the one who covered with gold' ('pon veinda perumal').[6] In 1118 Vikrama Chola (r. 1118–35), recorded in inscriptions that he devoted a year's state revenue to the enhancement of Chidambaram temple with gold, jewels and pearls. Among the many works, he 'covered with splendid gold the altar on which offerings abound, so that the light of heaven was reflected' (fig. 4), and 'covered with pure gold and adorned with numerous strings of large pearls the sacred temple car…in order that the miraculous dancer [Nataraja] who occupies the golden hall may be drawn in procession at the great festival'.[7] This display of seemingly unlimited riches was undoubtedly a genuine expression of religious devotion and meritorious patronage on the part of the king. It also cannot but have helped to impress the populace with this ruler's magnificence and remind them of the divine grace their ruler received from Shiva.

The popular veneration of the Tamil poet-saints served the objectives of the Chola rulers well and they encouraged the absorption of the saints into the mainstream. The Buddhist and Jain faiths maintained a presence under the Cholas and some of the processional bronze images dating from this period were commissioned by followers of these faiths (fig. 13 and cat.28). The Chola rulers, however, remained staunch and devout followers of Shiva, while tolerating and even supporting other faiths on occasions. The promotion of religious unity across the Chola territories by the Shaiva *nayanmar* furthered the process of political integration pursued by the Chola state.

THE PROCESSIONS

Public displays of temple ritual were an essential tool in this process. The most visible expression of this was the annual temple festival procession, in which the presiding deity ventured forth from the temple to be displayed to the people 'like royalty' and to establish sovereignty by marking out the territory over which the temple's religious jurisdiction extended. This maintained the role of the Hindu deities as at the same time universal, pan-Indian entities and gods with a strong sense of local identity, closely linked to the immediate topography through myth and magic. On these occasions, the gods were paraded, sumptuously robed, bejewelled and garlanded, to be celebrated in prayers, song, music and dance – rituals that are still performed today (fig.5).[8]

These temple festivals are known as *utsavas* – events to 'drive away sorrow'. Before the parading of the processional images of the presiding gods on animal vehicles (*vahanas*) or in temple cars (*rathas*), and the lesser gods and saints on shrine-like palanquins (figs 6 and 8), the icons are prepared by the performance of a number

Fig.4
Nataraja shrine, Chidambaram temple, Tamil Nadu. Contemporary print, purchased at Chidambaram, 2002

Fig.5
A troupe of temple dancers at the Brahmotsava festival, Rajarajeshvara temple, Tanjavur, c.1940

Fig. 6
Company school, Tanjavur,
Shaivite Procession at Night,
c. 1830. Watercolour on paper,
28 × 51 cm. Victoria and
Albert Museum, London

Fig. 7
Company school,
Tiruchirapalli, *Vaishnava
Procession with Festival Car*,
c. 1800, inscribed 'Sree
Rangam God set upon
Chariate'. Gouache on paper,
43 × 59 cm. Victoria and
Albert Museum, London

of royal courtesies (*raja upacarams*): the deity is offered betel leaves and areca nuts and then installed in the temple car, where a religious ceremony (*puja*) is performed in his honour. A mirror is provided for the god to check all is in order, and burning camphor (*harati*) offered. The ritual preparations complete, the procession can begin, to the accompaniment of temple musicians – an essential component is a troupe of temple drummers and conch players (fig. 7).[9] Shelters are erected to provide a rest point for the deity on the journey. Images of Shiva and Vishnu in their various manifestations are paraded, accompanied by their consorts, together with their offspring, such as Skanda on his peacock and the elephant-headed Ganesha. Lesser gods are also honoured in this way, as are icons of the poet-saints.

On special occasions, of which the annual festival parades were the most elaborate, processional images were embellished not only with textiles and garlands but also with lavish jewels, gold body covers (*kavacha*) and golden silks (fig. 3). In the present day, at Melukote in Karnataka, the gold– and jewel-encrusted crown and necklaces (*tali*) of Vishnu and Lakshmi are brought to the temple from the bank vaults of a nearby town under police escort. The first display of the god, in the temple's passageway, fully bejewelled and radiant, draws gasps of wonder from those devotees who are privileged to have access to the temple on the festival night (fig. 8).

Not all approved of such lavish displays of wealth and splendour. The Vaishnava saint Nammalvar (*c.*880–930) expressly decried the use of bejewelled icons, seeing such opulence as a barrier to comprehending the divine:

> Feet, navel, hands,
> chest, eyes, and lips
> red-rayed jewels
> set in a blue glow,
> and golden silks round his waist,
> my lord is all blaze and dazzle:
> I do not know how to reach him.[10]

The poet-saints provide numerous descriptions of these celebrated festivals, of the radiant splendour of the enthroned gods and of the rapture of the devotees. They, meanwhile, rapidly acquired a cult status and became themselves the subject of processional images.

The fame of Nammalvar, the most renowned and poetically gifted of the Vaishnava saints, was such that processional images of him were cast soon after his death and installed in Vaishnava temples across southern India.[11] He was venerated as the highest servant of Vishnu, to be honoured as the very feet of Vishnu. Today, devotees are blessed by having a golden crown (*catakopam*) momentarily placed on their head, representing both Vishnu's feet and the saint Nammalvar.

Inscriptional references to the veneration of the sixty-three Shaiva saints in portable form and in a festival context exist from the eleventh and twelfth centuries. In 1046 a set of such images was paraded at Tiruvottiyur temple, and at Tiruvenkadu an endowment of land was made to provide funds 'for bathing the god and the *nayanmar* at the mouth of the Kaveri River'.[12]

In the present day, at many of the richer temples, such as Kapalishvara in Mylapur, the ancient quarter of Chennai, a full set of bronze sculptures of the sixty-three *nayanmar* is still paraded through the streets on the eighth day of the ten-day Panguni Uttiram festival, held over the period of the full moon of the month of Cittirai (March–April). Each saint is borne on a small mobile shrine carriage, drawn by young male devotees. Special honour is reserved for Sambandar, who is believed to have performed a miracle at this temple, restoring life to a devout man's daughter, Pumpavai. His processional icon is singled out for its own ritual

Fig. 8
Processional icons of Vishnu and his consorts, Brahmotsava festival, Cheluve Narayana temple, Melukote. Photograph by the author, March 2003

lustration ceremony (*abhiseka puja*) at the temple tank during the progress of the procession (fig.9).

The Kapalishvara temple was chosen by Sambandar for special celebration in one of the verses he composed in the seventh century in praise of processional festivals. In 'Mayilappur' he described each of the major festivals held there each year, taking the opportunity in one verse celebrating the Peruncanti (Purification) festival to slander both Buddhists and Jains for their misguided beliefs:

> Pumpavai, O beautiful girl
> Would you go without having seen,
> at the Kapaliccaram temple
> surrounded by green groves,
> the festival of the Great Purification
> slandered by the naked Jains
> and the base Buddhists in voluminous robes?[13]

DEMOCRATISING WORSHIP

The production of processional bronze icons contributed to the elaboration of temple ritual activity and especially to the popularity of publicly displaying the gods. Festival worship always remained supplementary to temple worship, but its wide accessibility secured it a permanent place in the devotional life of south Indian communities. This allowed the populace to participate directly in acts of personal and public devotion to an unprecedented degree. The temple procession and the periodic festival parades outside the temple walls were the fullest expression of this devotion, and the portable icon was the key to this process of democratising worship.

Pleasing the gods was an overwhelming concern of priests and devotees alike. To this end, the commissioning of portable metal images became a major act of religious piety on the part of the Chola elite. Religious merit (*punya*) could be achieved through donations for the public good (*dana*). The presentation of processional bronze images to temples became an immensely popular means of expressing *dana*, as both sculptures and inscriptions bear witness. While only a king, marshalling the resources of the state and the spoils of war, could afford to build a major temple, others – lesser royalty and members of the nobility, ministers, priests, merchants, guild organisations – could all undertake, along with the king, the commissioning of processional icons. And,

of course, this encouraged public devotional celebration through wider opportunities for *darshan*.

As numerous temple inscriptions of the Chola period make clear, the commissioning of new processional images was an especially noteworthy event. At Rajaraja Chola's Rajarajeshvara temple at Tanjavur, built in about 1003–10, a wealth of inscriptions on the temple walls, pillars and base mouldings, records endowments, festivals and donations. This temple is unique in having in its inscriptions a detailed inventory that records the gift of sixty-six processional images. These were presented by the king and his family, including his queens, his sister Kundavai, and his great-aunt, Sembiyan Mahadevi, a renowned donor in her own right.[14] Of the total, twenty-three copper and two gold images were given by the king, including two icons of Shiva as Nataraja and one of his consort, Uma Parameshvari. A number of noblemen and the priest Guru Isana Shiva Pandita were also responsible for donating processional images. Each icon had in turn sets of ritual utensils and jewellery commissioned for their worship, all itemised in remarkable detail in the temple's inscriptions.[15] Of the sixty-six images listed, only two are known to have survived: a Shiva Nataraja icon and a standing figure of Uma-Parvati.[16]

Two further representations of Shiva Nataraja are preserved at Rajarajeshvara temple in the form of a mural painting, situated on the lower ambulatory of the main tower (*vimana*) of the temple. One shows the dancing Shiva icon installed in his dwelling, the *chit sabha*, identifiable by its distinctively curved and gilded roof; the other shows Rajaraja and his queens at worship, venerating Shiva Nataraja in his home at Chidambaram.[17] The siting of these murals away from public gaze directly adjacent to the temple's main sanctum (*garbhagrha* – literally 'womb chamber') suggests that they were a private statement of devotion by the king himself, signifying his personal allegiance to the Chidambaram Nataraja as his family's tutelary deity.[18] It is highly significant that Shiva is worshipped in this private mural as the portable icon of Chidambaram. The status of the metal icon had surpassed that of all images except the principal cult image in a Shaiva temple, the mighty aniconic, pillar-like *linga* residing

Fig.9
Processional icon of the poet-saint Sambandar being ritually cleaned by priests at a tank shrine during the Panguni Uttiram festival, Kapalishvara temple, Mylapur, Chennai. Photograph by the author, March 2003

Fig.10
Processional icons being ritually cleansed with ash and scented waters, Swetaranyeswarar temple, Tanjavur. Photograph by the author, April 1993

in the inner sanctum – the ultimate 'sign' (the literal meaning of *linga*) of Shiva.

In Shaivite temples today the processional icons, including those of the poet-saints, are usually housed in the pillared hall on the east axis of the temple, the *ardha mandapa*. They are visited there by devotees preparing themselves for *darshan* of the *linga* in the *garbhagrha*. In Vaishnava temples the processional images are typically installed in separate smaller shrines in the temple grounds, each dedicated to a different deity. Here they are the focus of worship by devotees who visit each in turn, performing *pradakshina* – ritual circumambulation – of the main temple and cult image in the process.

THE EMERGENCE OF THE PROCESSIONAL ICON

Processional sculptures are first mentioned in the devotional poetry of the Shaiva *nayanmar* of the seventh and eighth centuries. A vivid description of the processing of a palanquin-borne image of Shiva as Bhikshatana (Lord as Beggar), is provided by Appar:

> He goes on his begging rounds
> amid the glitter of a pearl canopy
> and gem-encrusted golden fans.
> Devoted men and women follow him,
> along with Virati ascetics in bizarre garb,
> garlanded with white skulls.
> Such is the splendour of Atirai day
> In Arur, our Father's town![19]

Appar names the festival day ('Atirai', the celebration of Shiva's lunar asterism, held in the month of Markali, December–January) and the location, Arur, an abbreviated form of the name Tiruvarur, a town in the Kaveri Delta. Interestingly, a major cache of processional bronzes, mostly of the Chola period, was excavated there in the 1990s.

A Buddhist source of this period makes explicit that copper was widely used for portable images at this time. In his first-hand account of Buddhist practices during his sojourn in India from 671 to 695, the Chinese pilgrim Yi Jing (I-tsing) expressly refers to the bathing of an image, be it 'gold, silver, copper or stone'. He continues: 'Copper images, whether large or small, are to be brightened by rubbing them with fine ashes or brick powder, and pouring pure water over them, until they become perfectly clear and beautiful like a mirror.'[20] Today, images in Hindu temples are cleaned with ash and bathed with scented waters just as Yi Jing described (fig. 10).

CHRONOLOGY AND DATING

While the literary evidence confirms the rising popularity of metal processional images in both Hindu and Buddhist devotional activity in the seventh century, the first securely dated icon comes from the beginning of the tenth century. This is a figure of Uma as Shivakami (Consort of Nataraja) installed at the temple in Karaiviram village, which, according to its inscription, was consecrated in the eleventh regnal year of Parantaka I, 917 CE.[21] The image exhibits an already mature Chola style – a sensuously flexed torso with finely defined jewellery and an elaborate crown. The folds of tightly drawn cloth and pleating of the tied waist cloth are particularly accomplished. This dated Uma provides the anchor around which other early Chola images can be placed in a suggested chronology. Processional icons survive that are without question earlier than this, but cannot be assigned a secure date.

Few Chola bronzes bear inscribed dates; far more common is the recording of an important donation in a temple inscription, usually carved into the exterior wall of the temple's sanctuary. Douglas Barrett made a convincing case in his pioneering *Early Cola Bronzes* (1965) for dating a number of major icons in this way, most notably the three images still used in worship at the Umamaheshvara temple, Konerirajapuram. This temple was built by Sembiyan Mahadevi soon after 969 during the reign of her son, Uttama Chola (r. 969–85) and one inscription, dated to 977, refers to the donation of funds for the special worship of Shiva as Tripuravijaya ('Victor of the Three Cities', a vengeful form of Shiva; see cats 3 and 4), Shiva as Vrishabhavana ('Rider of the Bull'; see cat. 13) and Ganesha, the elephant-headed son of Shiva and Uma-Parvati (see cat. 14). These great processional images may therefore be accepted as having been made and installed between 969 and 977.[22] But even if processional icons at a temple correspond with those described in an inscription, a degree of uncertainty remains as to whether they are the actual images or later replacements.

The tenth, eleventh and twelfth centuries proved to be periods of great prosperity for the Chola dynasty, secured through sound administration and the spoils of military campaigning, including naval excursions to Sri Lanka and insular South-East Asia. Much of this surplus wealth was spent on new and grander temples and on equipping them with devotional icons and associated ritual paraphernalia. Stylistically the processional icons of this period form a distinct group, exhibiting a consistently high standard of elegance and refinement. Sensuous naturalism is combined with refined gesture and posture to an unprecedented degree. Ornamentation in the form of finely detailed belts, necklaces, armbands and diadems may be assumed to reflect courtly adornment of the period. Again, few images are dated, but many can be linked with reasonable confidence to a specific reign through associated temple inscriptions. From the reign of Rajaraja through to that of Kulottunga I (r. 1070–1125), a series of high-Chola-style bronzes survive, reflecting stylistic shifts and the grades of quality created by the master craftsmen (*sthapati*) engaged in their production.

By the second half of the thirteenth century, by which stage the Chola dynasty was in decline, the luminous humanity of the high Chola style had given way to convention, with few artists able to maintain the standards of the preceding three centuries. The reasons for this decline can only be surmised: less generous patronage and less exacting patrons may have removed the pressure to perform. It is perhaps inevitable that the energy that produced works of such quality as the Chola bronzes of the tenth, eleventh and twelfth centuries could not be sustained indefinitely.

BRONZE CASTING

The twelfth-century Shaiva poet-saint Basavanna was exceptional in that he combined his extreme devotion with high office, rising to the rank of minister of state and trusted friend of the king. He steadfastly criticised those who put their faith in the veneration of icons and the following lines, written in the guise of a critique of image worship, provide a rare contemporary description of the lost-wax casting technique (*cire perdue*) used to make processional icons:

> How can I feel right about a god who eats lacquer and melts, who wilts when he sees fire?[23]

The poet here uses the process as a metaphor for misplaced devotion. This traditional metal casting technique is still practised today in the sculpture studios of India: the image is first modelled by the master craftsman in a wax resin, which is then enveloped in layers of clay (fig. 11). The clay mould is heated, allowing the wax to melt and be drained away. The space remaining, holding in its moulded form the impression of the original wax model, is filled with molten copper alloy. After slowly cooling, the clay casing is broken away to reveal the metal 'impression' of the wax model. The resulting image can be either solid if the model is entirely of wax and is therefore fully evacuated during heating, resulting in a 'direct-cast' image, or, if a wax skin is modelled over a clay core, then this results in a 'hollow-cast' image. In both techniques, larger images generally require the insertion of copper or iron-rod armatures to give strength to the wax model.

Protruding sections are later sawn away, but iron armatures in particular are often detectable, in the crown of the head, for example, marked by a small area of iron corrosion.

Much finishing work is then necessary. The ventilation ducts and casting sprues – the channels through which the metal is poured into the mould – form solid metal arms on cooling and these must be sawn off before fine chiselling of the surface detail and ornamentation. The *sthapati* is responsible for incising the pupils of the eyes, thereby giving life to the icon. Often this ritual is re-enacted at the temple as part of the consecration and installation ceremonies. The sculpture is then ready to be put into service as a processional image.

A rare example of an unfinished bronze icon, depicting the poet-saint Sambandar, illustrates a critical stage in this process (fig. 12).[24] This casting failed, leaving significant areas of the mould empty of metal. These occur along the back length of the figure, indicating that it was cast lying flat rather than standing. It retains still its casting sprues and ventilation channels. Despite the surface accretions on this sculpture, it is still possible to get a sense of the extent to which Chola bronze icons were cast 'rough' and acquired their remarkable subtlety of surface treatment and finely rendered details of costume and jewellery through a laborious process of skilful cold chiselling and polishing.[25]

Chola-period bronzes are generally 'direct-cast' solid metal and can be of considerable weight, ranging from 50 kilograms to in excess of 100 kilograms. An icon of Shiva as Vrishabhavana at Tanjavur Art Gallery is over 1 metre in height and weighs 120 kilograms.[26] Today lost-wax casting is practised in specialist workshops dedicated to making devotional icons. The village of Swamimalai in the Kaveri Delta remains an important centre.

Ritual purity was of the highest concern in the making of such devotional images and purification rules had to be strictly observed. The master craftsman was required to undertake abstinence rites before commencing work and to make offerings to the god whose image he was to create. Metals were seen as potentially powerful agents, to be treated with great respect, and auspicious alloys were prescribed in technical and iconographic manuals (*silpasastras*). In south India these dictate that the alloy known as 'pancha laucha' ('five metals'), should consist of an amalgam of copper, the principal element, with gold, silver, brass and white lead. Perhaps the earliest prescriptive text for metal casting is the *Manasara*, a medieval technical treatise in which purification rites, metallurgy, iconometry and iconography are all explained for the guidance of the *sthapati*.

COLLECTING SOUTH INDIAN BRONZES

How, then, did these beautiful bronze icons leave their places of dedication? A two-fold answer is given, again by Basavanna, who describes the vulnerability of metal devotional icons and the pointlessness of using them in worship:

> How can I feel right about gods you sell in your need
> and gods you bury for fear of thieves?[27]

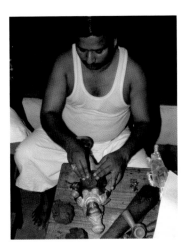

Fig. 11
Master bronze sculptor Sthapati Devasenapathy covering a wax model with wet clay, Swamimalai, Tanjavur. Photograph by the author, 2003

Fig. 12
Miscast icon of the poet-saint Sambandar, Chola, eleventh–twelfth century. Bronze, H. 28 cm. Victoria and Albert Museum, London. Gift of Professor S. Eilenberg

Stone images were more often vandalised,[28] whereas bronze icons were stolen for their considerable metal value. They were especially vulnerable to plunder in times of warfare. The invasion of the Tamil Nadu region in the early fourteenth century by the Muslim armies of the Delhi sultanates and their temporary overlordship at Madurai was a time of religious hostility and uncertainty. Many religious bronze sculptures were buried to avoid their being requisitioned by the Muslim occupiers and smelted, along with an immense amount of temple jewellery. Following the looting of Madurai in 1310 by General Malik Kafur, some '90,000 mans[29] of gold, several boxes of jewels and pearls, and 20,000 horses' were removed from the city's temples.[30] Madurai was perhaps the greatest prize, but other immensely rich temple towns such as Shrirangam and Chidambaram surrendered their treasures, accumulated over centuries of pious benefaction and meritorious gift-making.

Many of the finest Chola bronzes in collections today were recovered from caches of images secreted away in temple grounds and sometimes beyond temple walls in the surrounding countryside. Often buried hurriedly in anticipation of a Muslim raid, such images remained lost until accidentally recovered, often centuries later. Muslim accounts boast of large numbers of temple priests being killed, so it must be assumed that knowledge of the whereabouts of the concealed bronze sculptures and temple jewels often died with them.

These 'lost' icons were duly replaced by newly cast images in the centuries that followed. Since these replacement icons had been consecrated and put into ritual service, the temples had little need for any recovered icons. Often the temple's management agreed for such objects, surplus to their ritual requirements, to be given to government officials or sold privately. The Government Museum in Chennai has the largest collection of south Indian bronze sculptures, mostly acquired directly from temples in this way or through excavation.[31] A recent exception to this general practice is the case of the village of Esalam. After the chance discovery in 1987 of a cache of twenty-three Chola-period bronzes together with a fifteen-sheet copper-plate inscription fastened with a

Chola royal seal, the villagers promptly re-installed the images for worship. The copper sculptures were washed, clothed and garlanded and reintegrated into the ritual life of the village temple.[32]

The earliest recorded discovery of a cache of processional bronzes was made in 1856. It consisted of five Buddhist bronzes at the site of a major monastery (vihara) at Nagapattinam, on the estuary of the Kaveri River.[33] Further finds of Buddhist bronzes – in excess of 350 – have been made in the vicinity of Nagapattinam, many of which are now housed in the Government Museum, Chennai.[34] It is highly probable that a great gilt bronze Buddha in the Victoria and Albert Museum, London, was from another cache of bronzes from the immediate vicinity of the Nagapattinam Buddhist monastery (fig. 13). Of the highest quality, the Buddha is solid cast and heavily gilded and undoubtedly represented a substantial endowment by a Buddhist devotee. It would have been used in daily worship and the openings on the lotus-shaped base – for securing ropes – make it clear that the icon was also designed for use in parades. The image calls to mind a story about the eighth-century Vaishnava alvar Tirumangai, who stole a golden Buddha from the main vihara at Nagapattinam in order to fund renovations at his beloved Ranganatha temple at Shrirangam.[35] This outrageous act of religious vandalism, recounted with pride in the Guruparamparaprabhavam, the thirteenth-century Tamil compendium of the lives of the saints, was an extreme expression of the intense religious rivalry of the day, given voice in many of the bhakti hymns.

Highly significant finds have been made at the royal-endowed temple of Swetaranyeswarar at Tiruvenkadu in the heartland of Chola territory. Caches of bronze images were discovered in the vicinity of the temple in 1951, 1961 and 1979.[36] Cumulatively, these constitute the most spectacular and important discovery of Chola bronzes ever made, rivalled only by the Chidambaram hoard, discussed below. The group includes several masterpieces of the art of bronze sculpture, now housed in Tanjavur Art Gallery, of which the most famous, justly, shows Shiva as Vrishabhavana relaxing with his calf-bull Nandi (the latter missing).[37] This image is referred to in a temple inscription dated equivalent to 1011 (the twenty-sixth year of Rajaraja I's reign), which records that the piece was commissioned and donated by a person named Kolakkavan. The following year a companion sculpture of Uma-Parvati, named Uma Parameshvari in its inscription, was cast and presented at the expense of a local guild.[38] This was discovered in the same cache and may be accepted as the work of the same master craftsman and atelier. Also in the cache at Tiruvenkadu was a superb image of Shiva as Bhikshatana.[39] It is a measure of the importance of this icon that its donation was recorded in an inscription in the stone fabric of the *garbhagrha* of the Tiruvenkadu temple, which states that this bronze was presented by a donor named Amalan Cheyyavayer in the thirtieth year of the reign of Rajadhiraja (r. 1018–54), together with gold and silver ornaments and jewellery and lands to generate revenue to fund the icon's worship.[40] These were devotional images of the utmost importance to the ritual life of this temple.

In 1979 some eighty-seven bronzes, mostly Chola and none later than the early fourteenth century, were discovered concealed in a hidden chamber within the Chidambaram temple itself. This is the largest intact collection of Chola bronzes to have survived from a single temple. The find included a standing Paravai, consort of the poet-saint Sundarar, of unrivalled beauty.[41] R. Nagaswamy, then Director of State Archaeology in Tamil Nadu, who made the discovery, attributed the images to late in the reign of king Parantaka I, in about 950 CE. The group also included two large-scale images of the ninth-century poet-saint Manikkavachakar, who visited this great shrine to Shiva and composed hymns in his honour. Revered both as a *bhakti* poet and as a supreme teacher (*desika*), Manikkavachakar is shown holding a palm-leaf manuscript in one hand, while gesturing exposition or teaching (*vitarka* or *vyakhyana mudras*) with the other (see cat. 18). As Nagaswamy has noted, this saint, so well loved in Chidambaram, was honoured there with magnificent processional portrait bronzes less than a hundred years after his death, perhaps sooner. The bronzes found in the cache were reinstalled at Chidambaram after an interruption of nearly 700 years.[42]

Fig. 13
Standing Buddha, from Nagapattinam, Chola, late eleventh–twelfth century. Gilt bronze, H. 68.5 cm. Victoria and Albert Museum, London

As a direct consequence of Britain's colonial authority in India from the early nineteenth century until independence in 1947, high-ranking officials found themselves able to collect recovered bronzes through purchase and as 'state gifts'. Perhaps the most eminent such official was Lord Curzon, viceroy of India from 1899 to 1905. The cream of his large collection was a cache of Chola bronzes, reportedly recovered in Coimbatore district in the western Tamil territory of Kongu Nadu. This group formed part of the Curzon Bequest, which passed to the Victoria and Albert Museum in 1925.[43] Other major collections of Chola bronzes were formed by colonial figures, such as that of Lord Ampthill, governor of Madras 1900–06 under Lord Curzon's viceroyship. Most noteworthy was a group of seven fine Chola bronzes recorded as 'found in Tinnevelli district'.[44] The most recent, and probably the last, instance of this practice was a presentation made to Queen Elizabeth II on her state visit to India in 1960 of a graceful processional bronze image of Uma-Parvati (fig. 14). It was a chance find in the grounds of an abandoned temple at Sendagudi in Tanjavur district.

Excavated bronzes are easily distinguished from those that have remained in continuous use. The latter are typically worn smooth by centuries of devotional worship, including regular ritual cleaning with a wet-ash solution – a process that gently erodes and softens details, giving such images an ethereal beauty that enhances their other-worldliness. Highly polished, they glisten like gold.

Excavated metal images, by contrast, are less worn, and their decorative detail, engraved and chased, is still well defined and crisp. Depending on the environmental conditions of their burial, they often have a distinctive surface patina typically encrusted with earth and crystalline forms produced by mineral reactions. They generally respond well to careful mechanical cleaning, revealing the luscious green surface so admired by collectors.

The appreciation of south Indian bronzes continues to grow. It is a testimony to the vast production of such images from the Chola and post-Chola periods down to the present day that – beyond the living temples of south India, where these images play a central role in daily devotional life – museum and private collections globally represent this bronze-casting tradition. It is arguably the finest and most prolific tradition ever to have occurred in the history of metal sculpture making. Its aesthetic standards and technical mastery have astonished the most critical of observers, from the pioneering Sinhalese art historian Ananda Coomaraswamy to Auguste Rodin, a master of bronze sculpture in modern European art. With the trained eye of a craftsman, Rodin wrote in 1913 in praise of the Chola Shiva Nataraja from Tiruvalangadu:

> Above all, there are things that other people do not see: unknown depths, the wellsprings of life. There is grace in elegance; above grace, there is modelling.[45]

Fig. 14
Uma-Parvati, Chola, c. twelfth century. Bronze, H. 67 cm. The Royal Collection, on loan to the Victoria and Albert Museum, London

Notes

1 Literally meaning 'seeing [god]', *darshan* is a key aspect of devotional Hinduism and lies at the centre of temple worship. See Eck 1998.

2 See Stein 1978 for an analysis of the economic functions of the medieval temple in south India.

3 Rathnasabapathy 1982, p.xi.

4 Peterson 1989, pp.292–3.

5 'Chola-mandalam' was anglicised as Coromandel and is retained as the term to describe India's eastern seaboard, extending from northern Andhra Pradesh to Point Calimere in northern Tamil Nadu, approximating the territories of the Chola Empire at its height.

6 Balasubrahmanyam 1971, p.3.

7 Chidambaram temple inscription, in Sastri 1955, p. 345. For a discussion of the Chidambaram Nataraja, see Guy 2004.

8 For the role of temple dancers (*devadasi*), see Guy 1997.

9 Orr 2004, pp.45–6.

10 Nammalvar, Hymn 7.6.6, in Ramanujan 1993, p.30.

11 Ramanujan 1993, pp.xii–xiii.

12 Madras Epigraphy Report 1912, inscr. 137; 1918, inscr. 511: cited in Dehejia 1988, pp.39–40.

13 Sambandar, Hymn 2.183, in Peterson 1989, p.189.

14 Bronzes produced under the patronage of this remarkable queen were first identified by Douglas Barrett (1965) and grouped as the 'Sembiyan Mahadevi School'. The queen's pious philanthropy is discussed in Dehejia 1990A, chapter 1.

15 Venkataraman 1985, pp.152–62.

16 The Nataraja, still in the Rajarajeshvara temple in Tanjavur, is widely accepted by scholars to be one of the images commissioned by Rajaraja himself. Note that the *prabha* (aureole) is a later repair.

17 Illustrated in Guy 2004, fig.15.

18 Sivaramamurti 1974, p.223.

19 Appar, Hymn 4.21, in Peterson 1989, pp.184–5.

20 Takakusu 1896, pp.147, 150.

21 Nagaswamy 1979A; see also Nagaswamy 1995.

22 Barrett 1965, p.21. The author developed this study further in Barrett 1974.

23 Basavanna, Hymn 558, in Ramanujan 1973, p.84.

24 The figure is mistakenly identified by Pal as Krishna (Pal 1972). For a discussion of the child-saint Sambandar's identifying attributes – a cup of milk and an upward-pointing finger – see Dehejia 1995.

25 A flawed casting would usually have been melted down so that its metal could be reused. Why this one survived is a mystery. For a technical analysis, see Johnson 1972.

26 Rathnasabapathy 1982, cat.13.

27 Basavanna, Hymn 558, in Ramanujan 1973, p.84.

28 A few notable cases of stone images being appropriated as war trophies do occur in the history of Chola south India; see Davis 1997, chapter 2.

29 The *man* is an Arabic measure of weight that was widely adopted in the Indian subcontinent but variously defined; see Yule and Burnell 1886.

30 Elliot 1877, vol. 3, p.204.

31 Catalogues of the collection were published by Gangoly in 1915, Gravely and Ramachandran in 1932, Srinivasan in 1963 and, most recently, Kannan in 2003. See also New Delhi 1983.

32 Nagaswamy 1987.

33 Reported by W. Elliot in the *Indian Antiquary*, 7 (1878). See Guy 1994, pp.291–2, and Guy 2001.

34 Ramachandran 1954; Guy 2005.

35 Ramachandran 1954, p.15.

36 Ramachandran 1956; Nagaswamy 1960.

37 Rathnasabapathy 1982, cat.13.

38 Rathnasabapathy 1982, cat.13.

39 Rathnasabapathy 1982, cat.14.

40 Rathnasabapathy 1982, p.39.

41 Nagaswamy 1979B.

42 Nagaswamy 1979B. For portraiture in south Indian sculpture, see Aravamuthan 1931.

43 Nagaswamy 1967. See also Nagaswamy 1961 regarding provenanced Kongu bronzes.

44 The Ampthill collection was acquired by the Victoria and Albert Museum in 1935.

45 Rodin 1921, translated in Appendix B.

II   Beauty and the Body of God

VIDYA DEHEJIA

Youth who shines as a ruby,
as a cluster of emeralds!
Being who enters my heart,
stirring memory!
Come to me in my sleep,
be my friend,
give me refuge in your grace,
O dweller in Avatuturai!
SAINT APPAR[1]

LIKE A SENSUOUS Chola bronze richly embellished
with jewelled ornament, the god conjured up in
this vision of the seventh-century poet-saint Appar
is a captivating and youthful being with a dazzling
form. The bronze deities created between the ninth
and thirteenth centuries in the Tamil region of south
India under the Chola dynasty are among India's most
celebrated sculpted figures, hailed as exquisite artistic
creations. Indeed, across India, sacred images of gods
and goddesses, whether carved in stone, cast in bronze
or painted, share idealised slender bodies and enchanting
faces. This imagery is distant from that of the Judeo-
Christian world, and is perhaps related more closely to
the exhilarating imagination displayed in the Greco-Roman
era, when gods and goddesses were renowned for their
physical beauty. And yet the Chola images considered
here are among the most sacred in India, deeply
venerated by devotees.

The very concept of the sensuous as part of the
sacred, so emphatically emphasised in Chola bronzes
but a feature of images of the divine across the length
and breadth of India, seems to present a startling
paradox: can an icon imbued with divinity, approached
with veneration, be portrayed as adorable in a physical
way? How should the viewer deal with the allure and
intense physicality of the perfect body of a god or
goddess? Equally mesmerising and even more mystifying
are the images of the god Shiva and his consort Uma-
Parvati, or of the god Vishnu and the goddess Lakshmi,
portrayed as loving couples. Often, the god's arm cups
his consort's breast. Admittedly, they are partners in a
divine marriage, but the sensual nature of their imagery
seems to present a contradiction in terms. How is it
possible for sacred, worship-oriented images to be
so seductive, so stimulating, and yet inspire profound
devotion in believers?

The extraordinary visualisation of a gorgeous
sacred being, unique to the ethos of India, has its
roots in the concept of *bhakti* – a word that may be
translated somewhat imperfectly as an intense and
passionate devotion to a chosen Hindu god. Throughout
the ages, many paths of approach to the godhead have
been proposed in India. A complete renunciation of
the worldly and meditation on a formless divinity is
one. By contrast, the path of *bhakti* entails a joyous

worship that does not conflict with life in this world, and in which blissful devotion is expressed through resounding song and ritual. Generally *bhakti* goes hand in hand with the type of worship known by the term *puja*, which lavishes attention and devotion on images of the deities. The understanding of the one informs the other. Such was the practice of the poet-saints – the *nayanmar* and *alvar* – who travelled through south India from the sixth to tenth centuries, reciting hymns in praise of Shiva, Vishnu and their consorts. These saints and the *acharyas* (teachers) who followed them sang songs in which dwelling upon the beauty of a god or goddess became a method of asserting the deity's primacy, and thus an essential ingredient of *bhakti*.

SHIVA IMAGERY

Chola bronze images of Shiva as Nataraja, or Lord of Dance, confront the viewer with a vision in which divinity and sensuousness are inextricably mingled (cat. 1). The form of Nataraja – an exquisite face, elegant torso, perfectly proportioned thighs and legs, and gently curved yet tight buttocks – is indeed the epitome of physical beauty. In his dance of bliss, Shiva holds within himself the possibility of dancing the world into extinction, only to re-create it through the same dance. The flaming fire held in one hand portends destruction, while the sound of the drum in the other foretells creation. The dwarf-like figure upon whom Shiva is poised, Mushalagan, stands for ignorance and darkness that must be destroyed, and Shiva's other foot, raised, bestows salvation on the individual soul.

But it was not these underlying meanings that were celebrated in the songs of the Tamil *nayanmar* poet-saints. Leaving such interpretations to philosophers and erudite commentators, the saints, whose songs were directed at the average devotee, chose to express poetic rapture over the beauty of Shiva. Appar's famous poem dedicated to dancing Shiva Nataraja in the temple at Chidambaram states that so great is the god's beauty that it would even be worth forgoing the ultimate goal of severing the cycle of rebirth on earth to have another chance to gaze at him:

Fig. 15
*Shiva as Tripuravijaya
(Victor of the Three Cities)*,
c. 920. Bronze, H. 77.5 cm.
The Norton Simon
Foundation, Pasadena

If one may see his arched eyebrows,
the gentle smile upon his lips
of *kovai* red,
his matted locks of reddish hue,
the milk-white ash upon his coral form,
if one may but see
the beauty of his lifted foot
of golden glow,
then indeed one would wish
for human birth upon this earth.[2]

The popularisation of *bhakti* through south India
by the poet-saints coincided with the rise of the practice
of worshipping icons paraded in procession from temples.
The artists commissioned to create images of Shiva at
this time modelled his many manifested forms with a
skilled and sensitive touch. Stone sculptors modelled
deep relief carvings to adorn niches on the exterior walls
of temples and bronze casters produced portable images
for temple festivals. The productivity and expertise of these
bronze and stone artists is astonishing. Responding to the
steady demand from temple after temple, they created
innumerable images of the many forms of Shiva with
great sincerity and fervour. One such is a sinuously elegant
Shiva as Victor of the Three Cities (Tripuravijaya), standing
in an exaggerated *tribhanga* or triple contrapposto pose
(fig. 15). His face is a gently rounded oval with full lips
and elongated eyes. His matted hair, piled high on his
head, is adorned with his characteristic crescent moon
and a serpent, while a few escaping curls lie upon his
back and shoulders. An exceedingly slender torso with
a serpent peeping over his shoulders, and slender thighs,
neatly formed knees and ankles combine to create an
image of bodily perfection. The elegant gesture of his
hands represents his grasp of the now missing bow from
which he fired the single arrow that destroyed the cities
of the three demons.

Appar visualised the glowing form of Shiva in the
shrine of Kurankaduturai by introducing another
favourite theme, that of Shiva's sweetness:

My pearl, my precious gem,
glittering branch of coral, bright flame –
When I call him, 'My Father
who lives in Kurankaduturai
with blossoming groves',
my tongue tastes
an incredible sweetness.[3]

Appar addressed the god using everyday terms
of endearment such as 'sugar' and 'honey':

Honey, milk, moon, and sun,
youth crowned with the celestial white moon,
wisdom incarnate as the fire
that consumed the god of spring –
How should I forget him?

Sugar, sweet syrup of sugar cane,
bright one, brilliant as a lightning flash,
golden one, my Lord who glitters
like a hill of gems –
How should I forget him?

Sugar cane, lump of sweet sugar candy,
bee in the fragrant flower,
light that dwells in the light of every flame,
our Lord who loves flower buds gathered at dawn –
How should I forget him?[4]

While artists could express Shiva's beauty directly
by modelling an image of such physical perfection that
it transfixed its audience with wonder and delight, the
poet-saints often suggested the god's beauty indirectly
by describing its effect on those who longed to see him.
Appar's contemporary, the seventh-century child saint
Sambandar, composed several sacred hymns in the *aham*
mode of Tamil love poetry,[5] singing in the voice of a young
woman pining for her beautiful lover, asking the birds and
bees, the clouds and the waves, to speak to Shiva of her
love-stricken state and bring him to her:

O king of bees
you and your lady-love
are drunk with honey from the water-lotus –
your humming song echoes the waves.
Fly to the lord of sacred Tonipuram,
master of the Panduranga dance,
the lord who sports the crescent moon
and wears a necklace of bones
Speak to him of my distress.

O red-crested cock
who lives carefree in the green field
where tall grass grows
go to the sovereign lord of Tonipuram
where groves of *champak* abound
speak to him of my incurable malady
unfortunate that I am –
What blame is yours
if you tell him of my grievous state?[6]

It should be stressed that in the Indian artistic
tradition the human body is shown neither naked nor

Fig. 16
*Shiva as Somaskanda
(with Uma and Skanda),*
c. 970. Bronze, H. 58.4 cm.
The Norton Simon
Foundation, Pasadena

nude; it is invariably adorned.[7] Although sculptors made use of artistic licence to depict bodies seemingly bare, close observation reveals delicate folds of fine drapery at the ankles, waist, neck and arms. The perfectly formed body, male or female, is also decorated with jewelled ornaments and flowers, as well as following an entire range of conventions that may be subsumed under the term 'body culture', as coined by Daud Ali.[8] These include elaborate hairstyling and the heightening of the body's beauty by its anointment with oils, pastes, cosmetics and fragrances. Etymologically, *alamkara*, the ritual of adornment or ornament, is derived from the literal meaning 'to make sufficient or strengthen'; ornament is considered indispensable. The etymology of an alternative word for ornament, *abharanam*, is also revealing, since it means to bring near or attract (through magical power).

The significance of ornament in the context of India cannot be overstated. Ornament is auspicious and protective and makes the body complete, beautiful and desirable. To be without it is to provoke inauspicious forces, to expose oneself to, even to court, danger. The *Tirukkailaya Nana Ula* or *Procession of the Lord of Kailasa*, a ninth-century Tamil poem that has been translated by Blake Wentworth, emphasises this aspect of ornament. It speaks of young women warding off the unrefined with the anklets' beat, protecting their arms with armlets, sheltering their ears with earrings, girding their loins with fine dresses, and locking away their breasts in elegant bodices.[9]

A late tenth-century bronze of Shiva as Somaskanda, the name given to an image of Shiva seated with his consort Uma and infant Skanda (fig. 16), illustrates the vital role played by ornament in divine images. Shiva sports a tall, sumptuous, crown-like arrangement of his matted locks, a jewelled forehead band, numerous exquisite jewelled necklaces, a sacred thread of many strands, a high waist band, a richly patterned short *veshti* (waist cloth) held by a jewelled hip girdle, large ornamental

armlets, elbow bands, rows of bangles, anklets, and rings on each of his toes and fingers. Sharing the same pedestal, Uma, equally exquisite in form and ornamentation, is a fitting consort for her lord, while the infant Skanda stands between them.

Written perhaps a hundred years before the casting of the bronze, the *Tirukkailaya Nana Ula*, details the elaborate adornment of Shiva by Uma before his public emergence in procession. It would not do to be seen in public without appropriate *alamkara*:

> She adorned him with a garland fashioned
>   by the irrepressible god of love
> and dusted him with wholesome fragrant powders;
> taking up cool sandalwood
> prepared by ladies accomplished in their arts
> she applied it to his worthy chest.
> She clothed him in silk
> redolent with the scent of wish-giving trees
> and tied golden anklets about his feet,
> she placed a crown set with a radiant crest-jewel
>   on his head
> and on his forehead a shining plate
> sparkling with gems.
> She ornamented his ears with fish-shaped earrings
>   made of unpierced ruby
> and, taking up a beautiful diamond necklace,
>   a strand of gold,
> a well-crafted necklace of enormous pearls and
>   a shining
> garland of victory,
> she wreathed his holy chest
> and it shimmered in their light.
> She fastened brassards around his eight
>   mighty biceps
> and tied on a belt which delights all who see,
> she bound a waist cord about him,
> placed bracelets on his hands
> and adorned his body with elegant designs.[10]

The fact that Chola bronze figures were already richly ornamented in the cast bronze in no way prevented their further adornment with gold, gems, silks and blossoms. Tamil temple inscriptions speak of the vast numbers of jewelled ornaments given to temple bronzes, recording the quality and quantity of precious stones each contained and the weight of gold that served as a setting for the stones.[11]

To this day the practice of *alamkara* is an essential part of the ritual of *puja* performed in temples by priests before they open the sanctum for *darshan* – sacred viewing of the deity by the public. As Diana Eck has so effectively explained, through the purposeful act of gazing at the image and admiring its beauty, devotees make themselves ready to receive the transfer of grace.[12] The ritual adornment of Chola bronzes is such that they are more easily appreciated in a museum setting; when carried in procession they are so sumptuously decorated that their forms are effectively shielded (fig. 17).

UMA-PARVATI

The appreciation of a deity's bodily beauty was, then, one of India's customary approaches to the divine within the modes of devotion covered by the term *bhakti*.[13] Perfection of physical form was considered a prerequisite for the outflow of inner beauty and supremacy of spirit, and revelling in the bodily beauty of the divine was an integral part of the expression of love, devotion and adoration that is a concomitant of *bhakti*.

Such an approach was adopted by artists and poets in visualising and invoking Shiva's consort, the beautiful goddess Uma, known also as Parvati especially in northern India. Visual depictions of Uma invariably reveal her as a woman of great beauty, as in a Chola bronze of the tenth century from the Kaveri basin (fig. 18). Wearing a tall conical crown, she is a statuesque figure, sensuously modelled. Her full breasts are softly sculpted, with her skirt slung so low as to reveal the curve of her stomach, its illusory appearance of flesh contrasting with the details of the jewellery that adorns her. The bronze imparts a heightened awareness of form and a swaying sense of movement. The image is so evocative in its sensuous perfection that the viewer must remember that this is a portrayal not of any mundane courtly beauty to be admired for her physical perfection alone, but of the great goddess herself who is to be venerated and worshipped.

As early as the fifth century, Kalidasa, court poet to the Guptas,[14] celebrated the bodily beauty of the goddess, devoting fifteen verses in his *Kumarasambhava* or *Birth of Kumara* to a head-to-toe description (*padadikesa*) of Parvati's body.[15] Below are extracts from two of the verses:

Fig. 17
An image of Ganesha, decorated and adorned for a temple procession. Bronze. Kapalishvara temple, Mylapur, Chennai

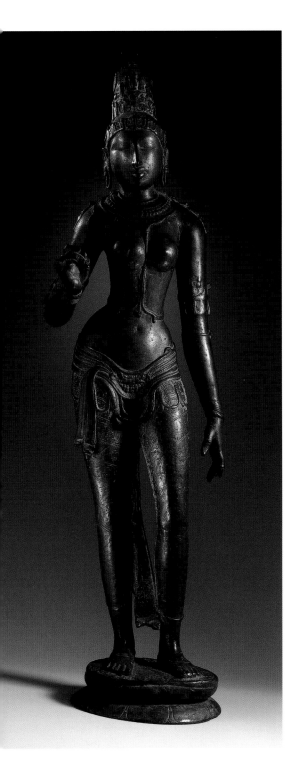

> She had thighs so lovely, rounded and even
> and long but not too long…
>
> She with her eyes like dark water lilies had full breasts
> and they were of light colour, with black nipples,
> and pressed so closely together not even
> the fibre of a lotus could find space between them.

The use of such language to evoke the sensuous bodily beauty of Parvati, as of Shiva, may perhaps be understood as fitting the style of royal court poetry. But such unabashedly sensual language is also used by the Tamil *nayanmar* saints in their sacred hymns, as in a song by Sundarar (*c.*800), in which he evokes Shiva accompanied by Uma:

> He passed this way…
> with the young woman
> whose mound of Venus is like a cobra's
> spreading hood
>
> He passed this way…
> together with the young woman whose soft breasts
> fill her taut bodice
>
> He passed this way…
> together with the woman whose smile is white
> as pearl
>
> He passed this way…
> together with the woman, perfectly adorned
> whose mound of Venus is veiled in cloth
>
> He passed this way…
> with the woman whose brow
> is the crescent moon.[16]

Sensual or inappropriate overtones were wholly absent from the mind of saint Sundarar, who saw only the divinity who was the consort of Shiva. Contemporary devotees, in turn, had such absolute and unquestioning faith in, and acceptance of, these saints, that they did not question the appropriateness of such imagery. Both word and image involve a complete, unusual and yet holy way of looking at the gods, a sort of controlled body consciousness.

VISHNU IMAGERY

In around the year 918 an exceedingly youthful Vishnu, standing in a three-quarters view, was carved by an unnamed stone sculptor to adorn the walls of a Chola temple at Pullamangai (fig. 19). The gently curved contours of the god's body are alluring, as is his face with its strongly arched eyebrows and full, sensuous lips. In his two rear

Fig. 18
*Uma Parameshvari
(Great Goddess Uma),*
c. 970. Bronze, H. 76 cm.
The Norton Simon
Foundation, Pasadena

hands he holds his characteristic attributes, the conch shell and discus, while one front hand rests on his hip and the other holds a damaged and hence indeterminate object. A distinguishing tall crown, forehead band, earrings in the shape of the mythical aquatic *makara*, necklaces, sacred thread, armlets, bracelets, waist band, hip belt and anklets complete his adornment. He stands facing the viewer, presenting himself as an easily approachable figure.

South Indian Vaishnavism (worship of Vishnu) envisioned five potent forms of Vishnu, ranging from *para*, the supreme form that is seen only in heaven, through his earthly avatars, to the *archa* or image of worship. Far from being considered a lowly form,

the *archa* image was thought to capture the essence of Vishnu and was considered 'a bit of heaven on earth'.[17] Stone and bronze sculptors across India created glorious images of Vishnu – tall, slender and elegant, wearing a high crown, a long *veshti* and rich adornment. These cult icons were addressed directly in specific temples by ecstatic poet-saints and *acharya*s who wrote that so great was Vishnu's luminous beauty and radiance that even gemstones sought to increase their own brilliance by being placed upon the image of the god's body.[18]

Like the *nayanmar* the Vaishnava poet-saints sang of the blessings of being born on earth to enjoy the beauty of Vishnu's image. Saint Tiruppanalvar composed a rapturous Tamil poem describing the beauty of Vishnu from head to toe, and the physical reverberations this caused in him. He is believed to have sung the song standing before the image of reclining Vishnu in the sanctum of the hallowed temple at Shrirangam. The closing phrases of five of the verses are quoted below:

> It seems as if his lovely lotus feet
> have come and entered
> my eyes!
>
> Ah! My mind runs
> to the red cloth
> he wears on his waist!
>
> The waistband around
> his lovely belly
> strolls in my mind!
>
> Ah! My mind is ravished
> by his red lips!
>
> My God! His lovely dark body
> of unfading beauty,
> strung with pearls
> and big dazzling gems
> fills my heart![19]

This passionate approach to the deity reached an electrifying climax in the poems of the twelfth-century poet-*acharya* Vedanta Desikar. Four verses of his Sanskrit poem *Ladder of Meditation on the Lord* demonstrate the application of the language of erotic love to a cult icon within the temple at Shrirangam whose allure has captured the devotee's heart:

Fig. 19
Vishnu, c. 918. Granite.
Brahmapurishvara temple,
Pullamangai, Tamil Nadu

III
O Lord of Ranga!

I see the exquisite curves of your calves,
the lustre of anklets bathes them in colours;

swift runners between armies in time of war,
long ladles to catch the liquid light of your beauty –

their loveliness doubled by the shade
of your knees:
seeing them,
my soul stops running
the paths of rebirth.

IV
They seem like firm stems of plantain
growing in a pleasure garden;

wrapped in the linen cloth, on fire
in the dazzle of the jewelled belt,

they are pillows for his wives,
Kamala, Bhumi, Nappinnai;

Ah! my mind plunges into the mysterious depths
of Ranga's young thighs

as into a double stream of beauty....

VIII
His half-smile, that just-blooming
flower, as if he were about
to say something – his pouting
lower lip, red
as a ripe bimba fruit.
His upturned glance, as if fixed on a distant
horizon, holds in one thrall
all those who long for an end to their grief –

this lovely face of Ranga's Lord,
adorned with a golden *tilaka* –

his welcoming eyes cling close to my heart
and will not let me go!…

X
So my mind touches the lotus feet of Ranga's Lord,
delights in his fine calves, clings
to his twin thighs and, slowly
rising, reaches
the navel.

It stops for a while on his chest,
then, after climbing
his broad shoulders,
drinks the nectar of his lovely face
before it rests at last
at the crown's flowery crest.[20]

Desikar's poem is an almost delirious contemplation of Vishnu as a temple icon. The image enthrals and mesmerises him, evoking an insatiable yearning to view continually the exquisite image of the god at Shrirangam.

The poet assures the reader that those whose minds are immersed in the glory of the god's body will not be born again; as S. P. Hopkins phrases it, Vishnu's beauty is a 'beauty that saves'.[21] In the signature verse,[22] Desikar speaks of composing his poem 'for those who long to climb, with ease, the hard path of yogis'.[23] The path of ecstatic contemplation and unswerving absorption in the bodily beauty of Vishnu is, then, seen as a path of meditative recollection, and one that is easy to follow compared with that of the yogis. It is accepted as an alternative means of approach to the god that is both natural and richly rewarding.

THE DIVINE COUPLE
As well as expressing the physical beauty of individual deities, the Indian artistic tradition, including that of Chola India, has taken pride in portraying the loving intimacy of gods and their consorts, whether it is Shiva and Uma-Parvati or Vishnu and Lakshmi. Their tender intimacy is exquisitely highlighted in temple after temple, in both stone-relief sculpture and bronze images. A deeply cut stela that once stood in a niche in the late ninth-century Kilaiyur temple depicts Uma moving aside bashfully as Shiva draws her to him with one left hand and fondles her breast with the right (fig. 20). Frequently, the god's left arm reaches around his consort to cup one of her breasts, while he turns her face up towards him with another hand (fig. 21).

In literature too, the conjugal love of the divine couple and their delight in each other's physical beauty was a theme for joyous celebration. As well as celebrating the body of Parvati, Kalidasa's poem *Birth of Kumara* praised the love of Shiva and his consort. Its eighth canto, entitled 'The Description of Uma's Pleasure', consists of ninety-one verses describing the lovemaking of the divine couple, commencing with the shy bride and following her experience. One verse presents a sensitive description of the new bride's discomfiture:

> Alone together, before she would let the robe fall,
> she would cover Shiva's eyes with both palms,
> but she was left troubled then by that useless effort
> as the third eye in his forehead looked down at her.[24]

India's vast corpus of copper-plate and stone inscriptions proclaiming royal genealogies and commemorating the gift of lands and money to a Brahman or temple introduces a parallel and even more intriguing phenomenon. Remarkably, the invocatory verses of these public documents frequently use overtly sensual language to describe not merely the bodily beauty of the gods but also their amorous interaction. This is evident not only in inscriptions from south India in the Chola era but also in those from throughout the country over the centuries. A stone inscription dated in the year 1163 from the central Indian site of Ratanpur, which records prince Brahmadeva's construction of a Shiva temple and other shrines and step wells, commences with this verse in praise of the god Shiva:

> May the divine half-moon crested [Shiva] increase your welfare! – [he] who has three eyes as if because of his desire to see simultaneously, at the time of playful amorous enjoyment, the pair of gold pitcher-like breasts and the lotus face of Parvati, daughter of the mountain.[25]

Bearing in mind the shy bride of Kalidasa's *Birth of Kumara*, it is an amazing conceit to conjure up so fanciful a reason to account for Shiva's third eye.

Copper-plate inscriptions of a ruler named Madhavavarman from the coastal town of Puri in the eastern state of Orissa, dated to the year 1164, were issued to record the monarch's grant of a village to a Brahman. They conjure up a similar scene of divine erotic play. The first verse invokes Shiva's matted locks in laudatory phrases and speaks of their dishevelled nature caused by Uma-Parvati's grasping his hair during love play:

> May the matted locks of hair of Sambhu, in which the particles of ash are separated by the overflowing waters of the Ganga, which are touched by the soft rays of the moon as if by white lotus fibres, of which the lustre is daubed by the red rays of the entwining snakes bearing sparkling gems on their hoods, and which are slackened because of their knot being set aside on account of Parvati's union accompanied with a grasp of His hair, protect you![26]

The many images and inscriptions invoking Shiva and Uma-Parvati during conjugal lovemaking beseech them to transfer their bliss to the devotees. An inscription of the year 1201 from Kalinjar in the state of Uttar Pradesh in northern India states: 'May Ishvara, who experienced the delight of an embrace from Parvati, multiply your excessive delight.'[27]

This Shaivite imagery is closely paralleled in images of Vishnu and Lakshmi, for example in a sandstone sculpture from Madhya Pradesh in northern India, which shows Vishnu and Lakshmi enjoying each other's physical proximity (fig.22).[28] Inscribed eulogies also celebrate with enthusiasm the lovemaking of the divine couple. The stone inscription of the twelfth-century ruler Madanavarman of the Chandella dynasty, which ruled central India, records the construction of a Vishnu temple and the building of a water tank by Gadadhara, minister of the monarch, using the analogy of the impress of colour by contact to stress the intimacy of Vishnu and Lakshmi. Engraved in twenty-nine lines on a slab measuring four feet by three, it provides a genealogy for both the Chandella ruler and for the minister. The second verse of the charter reads:

> May the undulating lines of paint…protect you, which, from the round breasts of the impassioned Lakshmi, transferred unto the rock-like chest of Sridhara, are like a beautiful eulogy, set down by the god of love in clear characters, a record of ecstatic amorous dalliance.[29]

Vishnu is frequently invoked as the lover of the Earth Goddess in his incarnation as the giant boar Varaha, who rescued the goddess when she was in danger of drowning. A stone image from the Queen's Step Well

Fig.20
Shiva and Uma-Parvati,
from Kilaiyur temple,
c.884. Granite. Tanjavur
Art Gallery, Tamil Nadu

Fig.21
Shiva and Uma-Parvati,
*c.*1113. Granite.
Amritaghateshvara temple,
Melaikadambur, Tamil Nadu

at Patan in Gujarat provides an emotive idea of this interaction, portraying the delicate figure of the Earth Goddess seated on Vishnu Varaha's raised arm, lovingly stroking his boar snout (fig.23).

The innumerable visual and verbal invocations of one or other divine couple in the throes of erotic delight were intended to act as prayers for the transference of their grace in the form of well-being, happiness and prosperity. This practice may be considered to parallel the transference of blessings through flower or food offerings, the *prasada* of temple ritual, which are returned to the devotee who presented them. However, with the divine couple the transference is more potent because the contemplation is of divine ecstasy evoked by eroticism.

It is in this complex pan-Indian socio-cultural, literary, religious and artistic context that the visual imagery chosen by Chola craftsmen to depict the sacred forms of the gods must be evaluated. The evidence suggests that the celebration of sensuous beauty in physical bodily form was an indispensable conduit to the appreciation of formless beauty and to the perfection of the spirit. The physical beauty of the bodies of the gods was seen as a path to experience the entirety of the god's pre-eminence, thereby attaining personal fulfilment and realisation.

Fig.22
Vishnu and Lakshmi, 955. Sandstone. Parshvanatha temple, Khajuraho, Madhya Pradesh

Fig.23
Vishnu as Varaha Upholding the Goddess Earth, c.1064–90. Sandstone. The Queen's Step Well, Patan, Gujarat

Notes

This essay is an abbreviated version of a chapter entitled 'To the Divine through Beauty' from a book in progress with the working title *The Body Adorned: Sacred and Profane*, to be published by Columbia University Press, New York, in 2007.

1 Appar, Hymn 4, 57.1, in Peterson 1989, p.213.

2 Appar, Hymn 4, 81.4, in Dehejia 1990A, p.39. The *kovai* is a climbing plant with red fruit, *Bryonia grandis*.

3 Appar, Hymn 5, 177.2, in Peterson 1989, p.210.

4 Appar, Hymn 5, 207.5–7, in Peterson 1989, p.211.

5 There are two modes of Tamil poetry: *aham* and *puram*, 'interior' and 'exterior', associated respectively with love and war.

6 Sambandar, Hymn 1, 60.1, in Dehejia 1988, p.48. This hymn is dedicated to the temple image in the town of Tonipuram. Shiva dances many different types of dance, one of which is named the Panduranga. *Champak* is a tree with fragrant yellow blossoms.

7 Nead 1992. Nead's 'Introduction' contains a fine discussion of Kenneth Clark's definition of 'the naked' as inferior and 'the nude' as superior, and examines John Berger's seeming inversion of these categories, with 'the naked' human as natural and 'the nude' as subject to artistic conventions.

8 Ali 2004, p.167.

9 Wentworth, pp.65–6.

10 *Tirukkailaya Nana Ula*, quoted in Wentworth, pp.51–2. The poem is traditionally attributed to Ceraman Perumal, the saintly king of Kerala, a contemporary and friend of the *nayanar* Sundarar, who lived around the year 800.

11 Washington 2003, pp.223–4.

12 Eck 1981.

13 The great Tamil poet-saints known as the *muvar* or 'Revered Three' – Sambandar, Appar and Sundarar – are often classified according to their *bhakti* approach to Shiva as child, servant and friend. All three approached him in the lover–beloved mode.

14 The Guptas flourished in northern Indian from the fourth to seventh centuries.

15 Kalidasa, *Kumarasambhava*, Chapter 1.35, 40, in Heifitz 1985, pp.26–8.

16 Sundarar, Hymn 85.2, 3, 6, 7, 8, in Shulman 1990, pp.539–42.

17 Narayanan 1985, p.54.

18 Hopkins 2002, p.205.

19 Tiruppanalvar, *Amalanatipiran*, in Hopkins 2002, pp.141–4.

20 Vedanta Desikar, *Ladder of Meditation on the Lord*, verses 3, 4, 8, 10, in Hopkins 2002, pp.157–60. Ranga is another term for Shrirangam. Kamala and Bhumi represent Vishnu's two consorts Sri Lakshmi and Bhu Lakshmi, and Nappinai is the south Indian equivalent for Radha, beloved of Vishnu's avatar Krishna. *Tilaka* is the auspicious mark worn on the forehead by Hindus.

21 Hopkins 2002, p.130.

22 The hymns of the poet-saints typically have a final verse, often the eleventh verse, giving the author's name and, sometimes, a reason for composing the poem.

23 Vedanta Desikar, *Ladder of Meditation on the Lord*, verse 12, in Hopkins 2002, p.161.

24 Kalidasa, *Kumarasambhava*, Chapter 8.7, in Heifitz 1985, p.117.

25 Inscription from Ratanpur, in Mirashi 1942, p.264.

26 Inscription from Puri, in Basak 1936, p.130. Sambhu is an alternative name for Shiva. Shiva carries the river goddess Ganges in his locks and, as the god smeared with sacred ashes (*vibhuti*), these are to be found in his dreadlocks too.

27 Inscription from Kalinjar, in Prasad 1990, p.75. Ishvara is another name for Shiva.

28 This image in fact comes from a Jain temple. Jain temples often carried a few Hindu images. Vishnu is closely linked to the Jina named Neminatha and both have the conch shell as attribute.

29 Inscription from Mau, in Kielhorn 1888, p.202. Sridhara is an alternative name for Vishnu.

III   Looking at Chola Bronzes

JOHN ESKENAZI

IN THE WEST, Chola bronzes can now be discovered not only in the seclusion of quiet and dimly lit museum rooms, where they seduce the viewer with their somewhat unreachable austere nakedness, their boundless energy confined by glass vitrines. In these recent decades of image bulimia they have become members of a postmodern pantheon of world icons, victims of an era of banality. Copies in every size and material, from glass to plastic, from fluorescent foam to marzipan, can now be found in markets and shops. They are no longer the exclusive preserve of publications on art and religion but are reproduced everywhere there is a need for a direct, unequivocal symbol of India: on travel brochures, comics, menus, T-shirts and in advertising.

Despite this desecration, Chola bronzes still exert an intense fascination for the Western viewer and the image of Shiva as Lord of Dance in particular represents the epitome of 'Indian-ness'. They have become a surrogate for India's most beloved and at the same time most trivialised characteristics – sensuousness and spirituality, elegance and fantasy and intense exoticism – exerting a deep attraction that does not require any intellectual involvement, based mainly on the evident and intrinsic beauty of the bronzes. Furthermore, they fulfil an anthropocentric view of the world as codified by Classical Greek standards of beauty, based on the human figure as the centre and measure of all things, its perfection synonymous with moral perfection.

It is the idealised forms of these images of the gods that attract Western viewers. The extraordinary fluidity of their bodies and disregard for realistic anatomical details enhances their abstract, symbolic quality and makes it easier to assimilate the surreal presence of extra limbs or animal attributes. Such details foster a fascination with the foreign. It is interesting to witness how this lack of realism does not intrude upon but rather clears the way for the appreciation and absorption of the very different moods that each deity personifies and suggests.

In Shiva Nataraja (Lord of Dance), the viewer appreciates the perfect harmony of his stance, his self-assuredness verging on arrogance, his suppleness and svelteness and his restrained energy, a combination of suspended speed and perfect relaxation – his muscles ready to spring, his body a reflection of the dance of the elements. Vishnu, the preserver, silent, noble and stable, straight and formal but never rigid, immobile and immersed in his role of Axis Mundi, emanates a reassuring sense of continuity. The viewer drowns in the soft, rounded forms of female goddesses, blushes at their sensuousness, while their feminine energy intoxicates and suffocates. At times though, they appear chaste and

Fig. 24
Victor Goloubew (?),
*Shiva Nataraja from
Tiruvalangadu,* 1911.
Photograph.
Musée Rodin, Paris/
Meudon, Ph. 16466

motherly, sometimes distant, unreachable or even merciless. Ganesha, Hanuman, Garuda and all the other gods suspended between the human and animal world enchant with their charismatic humour and their lightness, their primordial powers harnessed by devotion. In a similar way, the numerous poet-saints communicate respect, discipline, restraint and obedience but at the same time devotional 'madness', morally justifiable but free from all bonds of accepted behaviour.

All these different personifications and moods are generally characterised by similar visages, with huge, luminous, tranquil eyes, sometimes expressionless and oblivious to the viewer. Noses are long, fine and geometric with flared nostrils capturing a sense of time suspended, of that instant between inhalation and exhalation. Mouths are always large with full, generous lips, the shadow of a smile and the suggestion of murmured words of reassurance. The long ear lobes perfectly frame the oval faces although they seem surprisingly large, as if they might be a clumsy mistake.

Rich and complex jewellery adorns the gods – symbolically representing the enriched spirit – and scant and ethereal veils interplay with the fluidity of their bodies in motion, accentuating forms and casting shadows, forming hiding places to create rhythms of light and dark that caress and redefine the youthful bodies. They are forms in motion, with forces opposing, attracting and interrelating all at once in a never-ending dance, brought to life by a play of light that impersonates the energy animating their muscles.

In Chola figures the bronze alloy has somehow lost its heaviness, the static quality of Western sculpture. The flowing and supple forms are more reminiscent of the original elements from which the sculptures were created: the wax, water and clay of *cire perdue* casting. The different patinas, from black to silvery grey to emerald green, from azure to jade green, further enhance the impression of non-colour and non-matter – just a concentration of energy, constantly reverberating as though the viewer were looking into an iced-over pond. Here is a perfect combination of infinite vibrancy and a level of tranquillity difficult to absorb – an active stillness.

CHOLA BRONZES WERE CREATED at a time when religious art works were scant and their unique presence had the power to penetrate more easily and deeply into the viewer's consciousness. They embodied magical powers for the simpler souls, but they also stimulated the intellectual strata of the population by conveying profound levels of esoteric meaning through a complex vocabulary of symbols and allusions. Tranquillity of the mind was of course essential to everybody in order to allow transcendence.

Religious icons in India are created to sustain and encourage the devotee to transcend the limitations of the ego in order to achieve a higher level of awareness. This will eventually lead, through experience of the deity, to a better understanding of the devotee's own divine self and to acceptance of the human condition. Images help to harness the unruly unconscious so it can connect to a higher order that is reassuring, constant and readily perceived. In order to achieve this, the image is created in accordance with strict religious laws that determine every step of its conception and making. Precisely executed, these processes lead to a canonically perfect icon, which, if correctly worshipped, is temporarily inhabited by the deity, with whom the devotee can come into contact. In India the relationship between the human and the divine is very direct and physiological, simply part of everyday life.

The Hindu vision is based on the concept of Brahman, the 'Unbound', the manifestation of supreme consciousness as a boundless, vibrating energy in constant modification that generates, maintains and puts an end to every product of creation. The main purpose of Hindu religious art is therefore to develop the ability to perceive Brahman, the infinite aspects and actions of which are personified by an infinite number of gods.

The purpose of the artist is to give form to the divine principles. He can come from any class of society and can be considered a mixture of artist, craftsman, priest, alchemist and magician, whose role is to function as a passive channel for a divine archetype. His knowledge derives from intense religious practice and deep familiarity with traditional canons passed down orally from generation to generation.

In accordance with the tradition of the most ancient Hindu scriptures, the *Vedas*, the creator designs the image in a modular way, the basic unit of measurement being the face. He would generally consult a learned Brahman for advice in following the rules regarding size, posture, gestures, attributes, costumes, jewellery and facial expression. His models are the beauty of nature, the perfect body of a youth, the postures of sacred dance. He transforms undulating vegetation, flowing waters, majestic trees into full and rounded hips, bouncing breasts, long and firm thighs. Perfect rules combine with manual facility and, above all, an intense bond with the beauty of the intangible. At this point the sculpture becomes a manifestation of the same magnetic energy that animates and agitates everything that is alive.

The physical making of the bronze is punctuated by ritual and is the result of a subtle process that involves the fusion in different proportions of the five most auspicious metals: copper, silver, gold, brass and lead. When the art work is finished it is ritually purified and its eyes symbolically opened to allow the breath of life to energise the sculpture. Most importantly, this process allows the devotee to be seen by the god and the god to bless the devotee by seeing him or her in the ritual of *darshan*. The image itself is not the deity, it is a perfect form into which the divine temporarily descends in response to the correct invocation. This is an invitation to which the deity might or might not respond. Total devotion and purity of heart are required. The art work is then open as a channel for the dispersal of divine energy. At this point it will be treated as a living god, dutifully revered, awoken each morning, dressed and fed, residing in the temple and taken into procession to allow everybody to pay homage and to make eye contact.

Through love for the god and joyful devotion, the aura of the image grows and is constantly fed; it is kept alight like a sacred fire. Aura in Sanskrit is usually translated with the word 'sri', which implies lustre, splendour, glory, beauty, well-being, majesty and luck. It is to this aura that the devotee relates, not the sculpture's beautiful forms, hidden by the adornments of ritual: rich silk, spectacular jewellery, garlands of flowers. It is surely this aura, as well as aesthetic beauty, that draws the Western viewer to an unadorned Chola bronze.

APPRECIATING CHOLA BRONZES (or any religious art) in a secular way can ultimately provide an aesthetic, transcendent experience to the attentive viewer. A Chola sculpture is not a mere inert object but a work so rich in meaning it is capable of evoking manifold emotions and thereby effecting transformation at a deep level. Seen in a museum, removed from the framework of religion, the sheer beauty of these bronzes can be appreciated and understood sensually and not ritually. Aesthetic appreciation can be a means for higher knowledge and transcendence.

Through the skill of the creator classical Indian art achieves perfection – not only artistic perfection but also the embodiment of an idea, an emotion or a vision – and inspires a similar quest for perfection in the viewer. According to early Indian commentaries, the experience of transcendence is not the exclusive privilege of the devotee but is also accessible to the cultivated and initiated. As the eleventh-century sage Abhinavgupta said 'education of emotions through cultivation of aesthetic sensibility is the basis for liberation from the turmoil of life'. In other words, the joyous appreciation of art is not only an integral part of life: it can become a spiritual ascent.

Catalogue

with texts by Vidya Dehejia

1

Shiva and His Imagery

Tell me friend
what strange man is this?
His form is smeared with ashes white,
a serpent rears upon his hand,
in cryptic speech he seems well versed,
what manner of man is he?

Why look at his ashes
or fear his serpent
or heed his elusive
Vedic talk?
All you need to know is this,
he is the essence
the god of all
that lives and moves.[1]

S O SANG SAINT Manikkavachakar of the god Shiva, using the popular mode of a question-and-answer song (*calalo*) to acknowledge the paradox that the deity who is the highest of the high is at the same time the god of eccentric dress, ornaments and attributes. Shiva is the beautiful god of the matted *jata* or dreadlocks, which are wound together and piled high on his head. Adorning them are a crescent moon, a skull and a serpent, together with Shiva's favourite blossoms, the *konrai* or wild cassia and the *unmattai* or hornblower flower. On his forehead is a vertical third eye, symbolising his omniscient powers.

Shiva's attributes are a trident and a battleaxe, his weapons of choice. His favourite companion, an antelope, invariably accompanies him, often transformed into an attribute poised on one of his rear hands. He is the lord adorned with serpents; apart from peeping through his dreadlocks, serpents serve variously as his loincloth, belt, scarf, necklace, armlet, wristband or anklet. Saint Sundarar sang in fond mockery of Shiva's serpentine decoration and eccentric dress:

From pits and caves and lonely shrines
he catches snakes
teaches them to dance!
Had we known
the strangeness of his ways
would we have come to serve him?[2]

Shiva's mountain home is Kailasa in the snow-bound Himalayas, and his consort Parvati (daughter of the mountains) is likewise from the north. The sixty-three Tamil Shaivite poet-saints who lived between the sixth and tenth centuries relocated this god, together with his consort whom they called Uma, to the lush paddy fields, sandy shores and coconut groves of southern India, singing of how he chose to take up residence in the temples of Tamil Nadu. In the sanctum itself, Shiva is always represented in the form of a pillar-like *linga* emblem, but on the outer walls of temples and in the bronze images created for temple festivals Shiva took on a number of manifestations, including Nataraja (Lord of Dance), Tripuravijaya (Victor of the Three Cities), Somaskanda (with Uma and infant Skanda), Shrikantha (Lord of the Auspicious Neck) and Chandrashekhara (Lord Crowned with the Moon).

In contrast to images of Vishnu, seen by Tamil devotees as an actual manifestation of the god, a finely crafted image of Shiva is considered to be the perfect vehicle for the temporary descent of the deity during ritual worship, known by the term *puja*. The presiding priest invokes the god with an *avahana* or invitation to enter the image; when *puja* is complete, he performs a *visarjana* or sending away to permit the spark of divinity to depart. Devotees encounter the image after it has been enlivened and adorned and is presented to the world for admiration and worship.

Shiva's consort Uma is a figure of vital importance: without her constant presence no temple ritual is considered complete, since it is she who ensures that Shiva's beneficence is directed towards the devotee. In her own right Uma is identical with Durga, the warrior goddess, destroyer of a set of demons who threaten the stability and well-being of the world. Shiva and Uma have two sons, the elephant-headed god Ganesha and the youthful warrior god Skanda.

1 Manikkavachakar, *Tirucalal*, 1, in Dehejia 1988, p. 6.
2 Sundarar, Hymn 7, 18.4, in Dehejia 1988, p. 12.

1   Shiva as Nataraja (Lord of Dance)

Eleventh century
Bronze, 111.5 × 101.65 cm

The Cleveland Museum of Art,
Purchase from the J. H. Wade Fund,
1930.331

O dancer in the hall at Tillai –
the chiming anklets on your feet,
unmattai blossoms on matted locks,
your eyes' compelling glance,
the hand holding the drum,
body smeared with sacred ash
and clad in the tiger's skin…
all these fill my errant heart.[1]

1   Appar, Hymn 4. 81.7,
in Iyer and Gros 1985, p.81.
Translation by the author.

In his snowbound mountain home of Kailasa, Shiva is said to have invented 108 types of dance, perhaps to be identified with the 108 *karanas* or poses of Indian classical dance. Shiva dances in triumph at defeating demons, or for the pleasure of his consort. Through his celebrated cosmic dance known as *ananda tandava* or dance of bliss, he is believed to dance the world into extinction only to dance it back into existence as part of the cyclical time system of India.

As Nataraja ('nata' meaning dance and 'raja' meaning king in Sanskrit), Shiva stands in theatrical splendour on his bent right leg, while his gracefully poised left foot is raised high across his body. In his left rear hand he holds fire, signifying destruction, while his right rear hand holds a *damaru* drum, whose sound denotes creation. His right front hand is raised in a gesture of protection. Closely associated with the sacred Chola temple of Chidambaram, dancing Shiva, hailed by the French sculptor Auguste Rodin as the perfect embodiment of rhythmic movement, appears to have become almost a symbol for the Chola dynasty.

In this bronze Nataraja, Shiva stands serene and assured, master of the universe, within a circular *prabha* aureole framed with five-tipped flames that represent the oscillating universe. The god rests his right foot on the back of the dwarfish demonic figure of Mushalagan, representing darkness and ignorance to be overcome, who meekly raises his head to look up at the lord. The detailing is finely executed and the skull, crescent moon and crane feathers crowning his head are clearly delineated, although his matted locks, usually shown splayed out through the movement of dance, have broken away. The sculpture reveals absolute mastery of the art of bronze casting and exemplifies the mature iconography for Nataraja that remains the model today.

2 Shiva as Nataraja (Lord of Dance)

c. 1100

Bronze, 86 × 107 cm

Government Museum, Chennai

When he playfully began his dance
there proceeded from his twisted locks of hair
as they beat against each other with increasing speed
the water of the heavenly river breaking into spray.[1]

1 Umapati, *Kuncitanghristava*, verse 111, in Smith 1996, p. 12.

In this verse from a lengthy poem on Shiva dancing with a curved foot (*kunchita*), the thirteenth-century *acharya* and poet Umapati focuses on Shiva's matted locks as they splay out with the movement of his dance, spraying the waters of the River Ganges nestling within them. Once a heavenly river, the Ganges was beseeched to flow on earth so that the souls of humans could be saved by having their cremated ashes immersed in her sacred waters. Ganges consented, but requested Shiva to bear within his dreadlocks the initial force of her fall, which would otherwise split the earth. The haughty Ganges chose to descend with extra force and, to teach her a lesson, Shiva imprisoned her in his locks. This and other Nataraja images position the river goddess in Shiva's matted locks, portraying her as a beautiful woman above the waist with a flowing watery lower section. Nestling thus close to Shiva, the Ganges is considered to be his second love.

In this image from Kankoddutavanidam, Shiva dances within an aureole adorned with five-tipped flames, and his swirling dreadlocks, separated by *konrai* blossoms, bear goddess Ganges to his proper right. All Shiva's accessories indicate the movement of his dance. The serpent wrapped around his rear right arm sways to touch the aureole, his scarf-like upper wrap loops in the opposite direction, and the ends of his headband, knotted at the rear, also swing out to indicate his dancing movement. Mushalagan, the little demon of darkness and ignorance, lies meekly beneath Shiva's right foot. The authority of this magnificent mid-Chola-period image demonstrates its effectiveness as the emblem of the Chola dynasty.

3　Shiva as Tripuravijaya (Victor of the Three Cities) and Consort

c. 950–60
Bronze, 81.9 × 48.7 cm
and 65.1 × 16.5 cm

The Cleveland Museum of Art,
John L. Severance Fund, 1961.94

In a flash,
taking the mountain as your bow,
with a single arrow shot with a roar from the bowstring,
you burnt the Three Cities with their banners
to a charred ruin.[1]

1 Sundarar, Hymn 7, 9.4,
   in Shulman 1990, p. 57.

Ancient myth speaks of three powerful, dreaded demons who lived in three cities
(Sanskrit 'tri-pura') built of gold, silver and iron and placed respectively in the heavens,
in the air and on earth. Protected by the fact that they could be destroyed only jointly
by a single arrow, they terrorised the world. Their increasing powers troubled both
humans and gods, who appealed to Shiva. The god effortlessly performed the heroic
feat. A Tripuravijaya festival to mark this exploit has been held annually since ancient
times to ensure the protection of towns and temples.

This graceful Shiva and his consort, Uma, were probably crafted by a master
sthapati in the middle of the tenth century. Shiva's two front hands are poised to
hold the bow and arrow with which he slew the demons. Both images, displaying
an assured handling of form, are richly adorned and, although cast individually, they
are placed beside each other upon a single large pedestal. Clearly the result of sensitive
forethought and planning, the god and his consort sway slightly towards each other.
Both are images of eye-catching physical beauty and elegance. The eyes of the images
have been recut, having been worn down by extensive bathing and anointing over
centuries of ritual worship. It was important that the icons could both receive the
gaze of devotees and return a gaze of benediction during the ritual of *darshan*
or 'seeing' – the most important exchange between deity and worshipper.

4 Shiva as Tripuravijaya (Victor of the Three Cities)

c. 970
Bronze, 97.2 × 37.5 cm

National Museum, New Delhi

When the Himalayan gods surrounded our Lord,
strewed flowers, praised him, and cried, 'Save us!'
at once he graciously went forth,
to burn in an instant, with terrible flames,
the three solid citadels in the sky.[1]

1 Appar, Hymn 4, 73.7,
in Peterson 1989, p. 138.

This exquisitely poised image of Shiva as the god who destroyed with a single arrow the cities of three demons is, with its perfect balance of line and smoothly modelled form, a piece of outstanding craftsmanship. Shiva's hands are poised to hold the bow and arrow, now missing, with which he performed the deed. The pose is similar to images of Shiva as Vinadhara (Player of the Vina), when his hands hold the lute-like *vina*, also often missing (see cat. 7).

As is typical of Tripuravijaya, he stands in the contrapposto position, relaxed after completing his challenging feat, which required exactitude and precision. Shiva's face, with its full sensuous lips, is calm and thoughtful, and his matted locks are piled up in an exquisite towering formation, held in place with an ornamental tiara and a forehead band. Shiva's tall, slender body is richly ornamented with an entire range of necklaces, armlets, elbow bands, bracelets, a sacred thread, waist and hip bands, anklets and rings. The elbow ties and the knots for his hair ornaments, features that disappear in images of the eleventh century, suggest a date of around 970–80. This bronze is more grounded than the sinuous, exceedingly slender and slightly off-balance image of the god with his consort, cast to stand together on a single pedestal (cat. 3), but without the solid stability that marks bronzes of the eleventh century.

5   Shiva as Chandrashekhara (Lord Crowned with the Moon)

c.990
Bronze, H.51 cm

The British Museum, London

That crescent moon
brushing the top of the palaces
with their great cool walls,
circled by flowering groves,
crowns your matted hair,
lord of the great Ancient Hill.[1]

1 Sundarar, Hymn 7, 25. 7,
in Shulman 1990, p.155.

Although the crescent moon is one of Shiva's standard attributes, he is referred to as Chandrashekhara, or 'the lord whose locks are crowned with the crescent moon', when he is shown in an entirely benevolent form, far removed from his major feats of destruction. He is portrayed here as *kevala* (lone) Chandrashekhara, but is also commonly depicted with his consort, whom he gently embraces, when he is known as *alingana* (embracing) Chandrashekhara.

This graceful, richly ornamented image portrays the crescent moon (its upper edge broken) adorning the proper right of Shiva's tall crown-like arrangement of matted locks. A series of twisted curls representing the ends of his dreadlocks punctuates the multiple levels of the elaborate hairdo, while crowning the entire arrangement is an open flower.

The worn condition of Shiva's gently smiling facial features reveals that the image has been in temple worship for generations; details have been softened and blurred by the priests' hands rubbing down the image with a variety of liquids and unguents including milk, honey, sandalwood paste and sacred ash. Shiva's front right hand is raised in the *abhaya* gesture of protection and his left front hand holds the stem of a now lost flower. The attributes in his rear hands are damaged but it can be assumed that they were Shiva's characteristic battleaxe and antelope. The work shows the master touch of an artist working towards the end of the tenth century.

6   Shiva as Shrikantha (Lord of the Auspicious Neck)

*c.*970
Bronze, H. 58.4 cm

The British Museum, London

When the gods churned the ocean
with the biting serpent
and the mountain,
and the *kalakuta* poison arose,

you knew it would destroy the worlds:
so you swallowed it as your elixir
and haven't yet spat it out.[1]

1 Sundarar, 7, 9. 19,
in Shulman 1990, p.60.

2 Douglas Barrett, the former keeper
at the British Museum who purchased
this bronze, gave it this title. Doubts
have been raised as to the identity, but
no better suggestion has emerged and,
in view of the popularity of the myth in
the poetic corpus of the saints, the
identification is here retained.

This glorious image of a tranquil Shiva has been identified as his manifestation as Shrikantha, alternatively titled Nilakantha (Blue-Throated One), or Vishapaharana (One Who Captured the Poison).[2] The titles refer to Shiva's redeeming role as imbiber of poison at the time of the universal deluge of Hindu myth – a deed that challenges the supremacy of god Vishnu in his second incarnation as the tortoise. When the cosmic waters engulfed the earth and everything on it, the gods and demons decided to churn the ocean to retrieve the divine nectar of immortality. Vishnu took avatar as the Kurma tortoise to provide a stable base for their churning rod, the sacred mountain Mandara, around which they wrapped serpent Vasuki as churning rope. To the dismay of gods and demons, it was the *kalakuta* poison, too lethal to rest on earth or in the heavens, that emerged first. At the request of the gods, Shiva swallowed the annihilating poison, retaining it in his throat, thus allowing the nectar to emerge from the waters.

This exquisite and richly adorned Shrikantha, serene and noble, is portrayed as the gracious saviour of the world, seated in the position of ease known as *lalitasana*, with one foot crossed before him and the other lowered to rest upon a lotus flower. His front right hand is raised in the *abhaya* gesture of protection, while his other three hands hold his attributes – a battleaxe, antelope and rearing serpent – and the crescent moon adorns his matted locks, piled high on his head.

7   Shiva as Vinadhara (Player of the Vina)

c. 1000
Bronze, H. 76.1 cm

The Cleveland Museum of Art,
Leonard C. Hanna, Jr., Fund, 1971.117

He came
holding the *vina*,
the smile upon his lips
swept my heart away,
he did not turn back
to look at me,
he spoke enchantingly,
he came to Valampuram –
there he abides.[1]

1 Appar, Hymn 6, 58.6,
in Dehejia 1990A, p. 115.

2 Nagaswamy 2005.

With these eloquent words, the seventh-century Tamil saint Appar sang of an image of Shiva as Vinadhara, holder of the lute-like instrument known as the *vina*, enshrined in a temple at Valampuram in coastal Tamil Nadu. In this elegantly poised image, the bronze caster has captured the beauty of this manifestation of Shiva, master of music, who is hailed as the very soul of *nada* or sound.

Shiva stands suave and relaxed, his two front hands poised to hold the *vina* and his fingers flexed to pluck its strings, while his two rear hands hold a battleaxe and his faithful antelope companion. Half hidden in the matted locks piled high on his head are his typical attributes, a serpent and crescent moon.

A striking similarity exists between images of Shiva as Vinadhara, in which he moves his left fingers across the strings of the *vina* and plucks them with his right fingers, and those of Shiva as Tripuravijaya or Victor of the Three Cities, in which his left front hand effortlessly carries a bow and his right an arrow. However, the two manifestations are certainly different.[2] Several Chola temples carry stone relief carvings depicting the *vina* in Shiva's hands, making clear the slight difference between the position of the fingers in the two manifestations.

8   Nandi

c. 1200
Bronze, H. 51.4 cm

Asia Society, New York,
Collection of Mr and Mrs John
D. Rockefeller 3rd, 1979.30

'Let go his horn, Bhringin,
and Ganesha, drop his tail.
Ah, but you are sad, Nandi!
Poor Mahakala! Clasp not his neck.'
With such words being led to the feet of Parvati
may the bull with turning neck and dewlap swaying,
still looking at his three-eyed master who has lost at dice
bring you happiness.[1]

1 Abhinanda, in the eleventh-century
anthology of scholar Vidyakara,
the *Subhasitaratnakosa*, verse 77,
in Ingalls 1965, p. 70. See also p. 33
for the poet Abhinanda.

Thus did a ninth-century Sanskrit poet conjure up the cherished role within the divine household of Shiva's bull Nandi, here teased by Shiva's dwarf attendants, the *ganas*, prompting the goddess Uma-Parvati to come to his rescue. By invoking Nandi, literally 'Joyous One', to bestow happiness on the devotee, the poet also indicates the hallowed nature of Shiva's bull.

The god Shiva as Vrishabhavana (Rider of the Bull) and is frequently portrayed leaning against his bull mount (see cat. 13). Every temple dedicated to Shiva contains a shrine for a stone image of Nandi, placed directly in front of the sanctum so that the bull faces his master. However, images of Nandi rarely seem to have been included in festival processions. Bronze images are hence uncommon and those that do exist seem to have been placed permanently beside the stone bull. The holes in the rectangular base of this image, which would have accommodated poles for holding the sculpture aloft, indicate, however, that it was used in processions.

This seated Nandi has the distinctive hump of an Indian bull and his dewlap is indicated by striations in the bronze. His long neck is similar to those of images of Nandi from the Karnataka area, on the western edge of the Chola Empire. As the prized and sacred vehicle of god Shiva, he is lavishly adorned with jewellery, including metal covers for his horns, chains around his neck and foot ornaments.

9 Shiva as Somaskanda (with Uma and Skanda)

c. 1100
Bronze, 70 × 97 cm

Henry Cornell

Why settle down here
with the lady with the tiny waist!
in this town of Murukanpunti…

O why settle down here
in the town of Murukanpunti
together with the lady
with seductive breasts covered with jewels.[1]

1 Sundarar, Hymn 7, 49.1–5,
in Shulman 1990, pp. 307, 309.

Shiva is rarely separated from his consort, the beautiful goddess Uma. Devotees believe that in his manifest form Shiva bestows grace upon an individual soul only when in Uma's company. A bronze image of Shiva seated with Uma and their infant son Skanda (*sa* [with]-uma-skanda or Somaskanda) is regarded as the principal image that confers individual grace, and every temple, even those with meagre financial resources, possesses a Somaskanda bronze group.

This large and impressive Somaskanda image, with a delightful figure of infant Skanda poised in dance between his parents, is a fine composition dating from around the year 1100. Shiva faces the devotee in direct frontal view and sits in stately dignity in the posture of ease known as *lalitasana*, with one leg folded along the seat and the other pendant. Placed in three-quarters view, Uma seems to watch over infant Skanda. Shiva's right front hand makes the gesture of benediction and the left is poised in a graceful gesture, while his two rear hands hold the battleaxe and the antelope. A crescent moon crowns his tall matted locks and he is richly adorned, as is Uma, who wears a tall conical crown. This monumental Somaskanda bronze was clearly commissioned for a major temple by a wealthy, maybe royal, devotee.

10 Devi Uma Parameshvari (Great Goddess Uma)

c. 1012
Bronze, H. 88.9 cm

Asia Society, New York,
Collection of Mr and Mrs
John D. Rockefeller 3rd, 1979.19

Fresh as newborn lotus buds,
lustrous as *kongu* blossoms,
honeyed like young coconuts,
golden *kalashas* filled
with the nectar of the gods,
are the breasts of the resplendent Uma.[1]

1 Sambandar, Hymn 260, 4, in Dehejia
1988, p.45. This hymn is actually
addressed to the conjoint form of
Shiva and Uma known as Ardhanari
but Sambandar chose to emphasise
Uma without any description of Shiva.
A 'kalasha' is a vase – symbol of
abundance, wisdom and immortality,
containing the nectar of eternal life.

2 Sambandar, Hymn 260,
3, in Dehejia 1988, p.44.

3 Dehejia 1990A, p.67, plate 53.

Uma Parameshvari, or Great Goddess Uma as she is addressed in Tamil Nadu –
in contrast to the more northern, Sanskrit title of Parvati – is always portrayed by artists
as a slender, seductive and exquisitely beautiful woman. The Tamil saints describe her
in their sacred hymns in what seems, to modern ears, remarkably sensual language,
as in the verse quoted above from a hymn by the seventh-century child saint Sambandar,
which also includes the following lines:

Smooth and curved
her mound of Venus
like the snake's dancing hood.
Her flawless gait
mocks the peacock's grace.
Feet soft as cotton down
and waist a slender creeper.[2]

In bronze temple assemblages Uma is represented in a variety of subtly different
guises, both on her own and to accompany Shiva in one or other of his manifestations.
Without Uma's presence in temple rites, no ritual is considered complete.

This bronze Uma stands in a graceful *tribhanga* posture. Her right hand is raised
to hold a lotus or blue lily blossom (missing today). The fluent outline of her slim body
and the gentle naturalistic curve of her breasts, especially evident in profile, are closely
similar to the famous Tiruvenkadu bronze of the year 1012, created towards the end
of the reign of the Chola king Rajaraja (r. 985–1014).[3] Uma is richly adorned, and the
clearly defined decorative details contrast with the smoothly modelled planes of her
body to suggest an illusion of flesh. The sensuous quality of the image is the visual
counterpart of the vivid phraseology used by the Tamil saints to celebrate the bodily
perfection of the goddess.

11   Durga

c.970
Bronze, 57.2 × 20 cm

Brooklyn Museum, New York, Gift of
Georgia and Michael de Havenon in
memory of William H. Wolff, 1992.142

O King, a certain woman dwells [there],
exceptionally beautiful, causing the Himalayas to glow.
Such a form has never been seen anywhere by anyone.
You should find out who this goddess is and seize her, O king!
She is a jewel among women; with the most beautiful limbs,
illuminating all directions with her lustre.[1]

1 *Glory of the Goddess*, chapter 5,
10–12, in Coburn 1991, pp.55–6.

In the sixth-century text, *Glory of the Goddess*, this was how the demon generals Canda and Munda described the warrior goddess Durga to their master, Sumbha. Artists sculpting her image in stone or bronze likewise created a vision of divine radiance. She is the goddess addressed as Uma-Parvati in her more passive role as consort and constant companion of Shiva. As the powerful Durga, however, she is the Impassable One, destroyer of demonic forces that threaten the universe, renowned for slaying the buffalo demon. She is invoked for protection and for this reason is often placed at the entrance of palaces, forts and temples. In Tamil Nadu, she is believed to be the sister of god Vishnu and is often shown with his attributes of discus and conch shell, as in this example. Thus, while images of Durga are found more often in the context of a Shiva temple, she is also at home in a Vaishnava context.

This exquisite tenth-century bronze presents Durga as an exceptionally poised and slender goddess, her supple body projecting a youthful image. She stands resolutely upright, resting her weight equally on both feet, in contrast to the contrapposto pose typically used in depictions of Uma. She wears a rich array of ornaments including a sacred thread, necklaces, armlets, bangles and anklets, raising her front right hand in the *abhaya* gesture of protection and resting her left hand on her thigh. Comparison with dated images suggests that this icon was created in the third quarter of the tenth century, perhaps around the year 970.

12 Bhadrakali

c. 1250
Bronze, 75.4 × 30.5 cm

National Museum, New Delhi

Mind and words are powerless
to encompass your glory
whose extent is as immeasurable
as that of cosmic space;
The myriads of galaxies you set in motion
move with precipitous speed;
Were the earth to be split into atoms
and set end to end
that immense distance would be equal
to that you have placed between universes.
O beautiful one,
I extol you as Kali.[1]

1 Subramania Bharati, 'Invocation to Mahashakti', verse 1, in Dehejia 1999.

Imposing in her statuesque grandeur, Devi Uma in her fierce form as Bhadrakali, or Auspicious Kali, stands with both feet planted firmly on the ground. The word 'kali' has ominous connotations, meaning both 'dark one' and 'time', which devours all things. She is a warrior goddess, destroyer of demons. But her smiling face, missing Bhadrakali's characteristic fangs, reassures the worshipper, as do her two front hands, one raised in the gesture of protection and the other slightly lowered in the wish-granting gesture. Her two rear hands hold an elephant goad and the remains of a noose, both weapons with which she redeems sinners by destroying their evil deeds.

Bhadrakali's hair, arranged as a flaming halo, is adorned with a skull and Shiva's crescent moon, emphasising her status as his consort in her quiescent mood. Her finely pleated long skirt clings to her limbs and its folded ends cascade down the sides of her legs. She is richly adorned with all manner of ornament. The three lines along her ribcage are a sign of female beauty: a woman with this attribute was applauded in poetry as 'trivali tarangini', or 'she with the three waves [on her stomach]'. The firm treatment of her ribcage and the general sharpness of detail suggest workmanship from towards the end of the Chola period.

In her aspect as cosmic energy, the goddess remains a powerful force in south India, as indicated by the early twentieth-century Tamil poem by Subramania Bharati quoted above.

13 Trident with Shiva as Vrishabhavana (Rider of the Bull)

*c.*950

Bronze, H.83.6 cm

The British Museum, London

How shines before my eyes his brilliant trident!
How gleams the crescent moon atop his lengthy locks!
How heavy the scent of *konrai* garland!
How bright the glow of conch shell and *thodu*![1]

1 Appar, Hymn 6. 137. 18. 1, in Dehejia 1988, p.33. A *thodu* is an ear stud.

2 Davis 1991, p.117.

3 Dehejia 1990A, p.67, plate 50.

Shiva wields the trident as a lethal weapon in a range of feats of cosmic destruction: with it he impales the demon of darkness (Andhaka), the god of death (Yama), time itself (Kala). Its shimmering presence is enough to strike terror into demons and glee into the hearts of devotees like the poet-saint Appar, who sang the verse quoted above. But it was not this role as weapon of destruction that was celebrated in the many tridents commissioned by the temples of Chola India. Rather, the trident acquired a deep philosophical meaning and devotees were told to think of it as a weapon of grace with which Shiva destroyed the bonds that keep captive the human soul in an unending cycle of rebirth.[2] Bronze tridents were created, either unadorned or with varying images of Shiva or the goddess Uma featured against their prongs, for use in a ritual known as *ayudha puja* or weapon worship, which became a regular feature of temple rites.

Shiva is renowned as the Rider of the Bull. Here he is positioned against a finely fashioned trident, leaning gracefully against his bull mount, Nandi, with one elbow resting upon its head. Like the famous dated image of 1011 from Tiruvenkadu,[3] Shiva has one foot crossed in front of the other and his hair is styled casually rather than in the typical crown-like way. The sinuous elegance of this relaxed image suggests a date of around 950, a half-century prior to the Tiruvenkadu image. The worn nature of the bronze, with Shiva's facial features largely obliterated, testifies to centuries of ritual bathing and anointing in a manner similar to that undertaken to this day by temple priests in Tamil Nadu.

14 Ganesha

c.1070
Bronze, H.50.2 cm

The Cleveland Museum of Art,
Gift of Katharine Holden Thayer,
1970.62

I praise the elephant-faced giver of boons…
Whose trunk curves as the sacred syllable Om,
with crescent moon on his forehead,
sugar-cane staff in left hand
and pomegranate and noose in his lotus hand
without blemish, shaped like a giant
whose rounded form is pleasing.[1]

1 Adapted from a well-known song composed by the nineteenth-century musician Muthuswami Dikshitar, one of a revered trio responsible for the revival of southern Indian classical music; see Catlin 1991. In varying traditions Ganesha holds different fruits, sometimes the mango and sometimes a 'seed-filled' fruit, interpreted as the pomegranate.

The delightful pot-bellied Ganesha, with his elephant head and curved trunk, is perhaps the most endearing and gentle of gods. He is the elder son of Shiva and Uma Parvati. Various legends exist to explain his elephant head. One speaks of the proud young mother Uma-Parvati asking the planetary deity Shani, or Saturn, to admire her child, forgetting that his glance withered all he saw. At the god Brahma's urging, Uma replaced the child's head with that of the first living creature to pass by, which happened to be an elephant. An alternative story speaks of Uma-Parvati leaving Ganesha to guard the door while she took a bath, instructing him to let in no one. When Shiva himself was refused entry, he cut off Ganesha's head but, rueing his deed, vowed to replace it with the head of the first being he saw.

This crowned and richly adorned image displays powerful modelling. Standing Ganesha holds a battleaxe and noose (to cut the bonds of rebirth) in his two rear hands, while the two front hands hold his own tusk (broken off in a victorious battle against a mighty demon) and a sweet confection (*modaka*) – his love of sweets is proverbial.

Ganesha is famed for warding off obstacles and is thus the propitious god of new beginnings, to be worshipped at the start of any new venture. A scribe in India putting pen to fresh paper will first inscribe the word 'Ganesha', as will students commencing an exam. When preparing sweets for a festival day, the first confection will be set aside in the name of Ganesha. He is addressed also as Ganapati – leader (*pati*) of Shiva's dwarf-like *gana* attendants.

2

Shiva Saints

BETWEEN THE SIXTH and tenth centuries there arose a community of holy persons who travelled the Tamil-speaking region of south India stopping at temple after temple to sing the glories of the images of Shiva or Vishnu enshrined within. Those who dedicated their lives to Shiva were known as *nayanmar* or 'leaders', while those who worshipped Vishnu were known as *alvar* or 'those who are immersed [in the divine]'. These saints introduced a particularly intense and emotional mode of devotion – *bhakti* – to their god, an approach that saw the deity in more human terms and that fostered the creation of portable images of the gods that could be paraded outside the temples to be worshipped by the masses. The saints in turn became the subjects of such sculptures themselves.

Around the year 800 Shaiva saint Sundarar composed a song naming sixty-two holy persons, and he was added to the list to constitute a group of sixty-three *nayanmar*. Their poems were collected in the seven-volume *Tevaram*. Three of the group – child saint Sambandar, Appar and Sundarar, whose verses appear throughout the catalogue entries – were known as the *muvar* or 'Revered Three' and composed some seven hundred hymns. The poems of the later, ninth-century saint Manikkavachakar made such an impact that a new grouping known as the *nalvar* or 'Revered Four' came into being. Three women were among the sixty-three Shaiva saints. Not all of these *nayanmar* were historical personages, in contrast to the Vaishnava saints, all twelve of whom appear to have been historical figures.

The Tamil saints continue to this day to inspire affection and devotion among Tamilians, and their hymns are still chanted daily in the temples. In Shiva temples, bronze images of all sixty-three *nayanmar* are placed in the hall immediately surrounding the sanctum where they are lustrated, clothed and ornamented in a manner similar to the deity himself. An inscription testifies to a festival of the sixty-three Shaiva saints being held at least as early as the year 1040 at the Tiruvottiyur temple just outside Chennai.[1] Comparable festivals continue to be celebrated at the Mylapur temple in the city.

1 *MER* 1912, no. 137.

15 Saint Sambandar

c. 1050–75
Bronze, H. 60 cm

Dr Siddharth Bhansali, New Orleans

Out of your compassion
O daughter of the mountain
you gave your milk
to the dravida child,
having drunk it
did he not write enchanting verse
becoming the greatest of poets![1]

1 *Saundaryalahari*, Hymn 40.75, in Subramaniam 1977. Subramaniam incorrectly identifies the southern child mentioned in the poem as its author, supposedly Sankara, rather than as Sambandar, who is surely the subject of the verse.

With these words the author of a famous poem glorifying the goddess Uma, the *Saundaryalahiri* or *Waves of Beauty*, made reference to the seventh-century child saint Sambandar. Hagiographic legend speaks of the Brahman infant being taken regularly to the temple by his father. On one occasion, having been left on the steps of the temple tank while his father went in for a ritual dip, Sambandar began to cry with hunger. His father returned to find him with milk running down his chin, playing with a golden cup. When asked who had given him the milk, the child pointed to the temple tower where there was an image of the goddess Uma seated beside Shiva.

It is this incident that is commemorated in this bronze image of Sambandar, depicted as a charming little naked infant with an empty cup in one hand, while he points upwards with the other. Standing in gentle contropposto, he is adorned with the traditional waist string, a simple necklace, bangles and anklets. This engaging image capturing the appeal of the child Sambandar is typical of the style of the Kaveri Delta region in the Chola heartland.

16 Saint Sambandar

c. 1250
Bronze, 42 × 22 cm

Linden-Museum, Stuttgart

O fellow devotees!
Kurralam, on the tall slopes
of whose fragrant hill
striped bees make music
in woods full of *venkai* trees
is the fair town beloved of our Lord,
who wears the blooming *konrai* wreath,
and likes to bathe in sweet milk and ghee! [1]

1 Sambandar, Hymn 1, 99.1, in Peterson 1989, p. 171.

2 Dehejia 1995, especially pp. 142–5.

So sang the seventh-century child saint Sambandar of Shiva, whom he describes not in his traditional home in the northern Himalayas but in Tamil Nadu's countryside with its richly wooded hills and flowering trees abounding with flora and fauna. While several of Sambandar's songs contain philosophical or mythical content, a larger number are devoted entirely to a joyous expression of the beauty and glory of Shiva and Uma in the context of nature. Sambandar was also largely responsible for the revival of Tamil musical poetry or *isai*: he sang over four thousand verses, all set to music, accompanied by a fellow saint on the *yal*, an ancient lute-like instrument.

Perhaps it was his celebratory approach, together with his love of music, that suggested to artists that Sambandar should be portrayed dancing. His left hand is poised in a graceful dance gesture while the index finger of the right hand points upwards – an iconographical trademark relating to the legend that, when a cup of milk miraculously appeared in the hand of the hungry young Sambandar, he pointed to an image of Uma as his source of nourishment. The bronze is otherwise similar in iconography to images of dancing child god Krishna, Vishnu's ninth incarnation, whose popularity probably prompted artists to create an image of equal appeal in a Shaiva context. [2] The angularity of form and sharpness of detail suggest a date towards the end of the Chola period.

17 Saint Karaikkal Ammaiyar

Twelfth century
Copper alloy, 23.2 × 16.5 cm

Sagging breasts and swollen veins,
protruding eyes, bare white teeth and sunken belly,
reddened hair and pointed teeth,
skeletal legs and knobbly knees
has this female ghoul.[1]

1 Karaikkal Ammaiyar,
Tiruvalankadu Muttha Tirupadikam, 1,
in Dehejia 1988, p. 118.

Thus sang Karraikal Ammaiyar of herself in a poem she wrote celebrating Shiva. Such descriptions, together with the legend of her life, were responsible for the bizarre imagery created by artists of a gaunt, emaciated saint. She lived in the coastal town of Karaikkal sometime in the sixth century and was one of three women among the sixty-three Shaiva *nayanmar*.

As the young and beautiful Punitavati, the saint was a devout worshipper of Shiva, with her husband Paramadatta. Her story revolves around a divine mango that appeared in her hand when she invoked Shiva, only to vanish when her husband reached out to take it. Paramadatta, disturbed by Punitavati's powers, abandoned her. Released from all wifely obligations, Punitavati beseeched Shiva to divest her of the burden of her flesh and asked only that she be able to watch him dance into eternity. In place of the young woman there miraculously appeared an emaciated hag, known thenceforth as Mother of Karaikkal or Karaikkal Ammaiyar.

This evocative bronze portrays the saint not so much as a ghoulish figure but rather as a once-beautiful woman who has lost her flesh, leaving her with a skeletal appearance. Her swinging breasts, almost menacing in their sharp outline, descend from starkly delineated collarbones. Her bony ribcage is plainly visible from the rear, as is the exaggerated curve of her hunched back. Yet, her calm, smiling face expresses her inner peace as she blissfully plays her cymbals and sings to the glory of Shiva, her dancing lord.

18   Saint Manikkavachakar

c. 1100

Bronze, 50.2 × 21.8 cm

National Museum, New Delhi

O Lord Shiva
on that day when you looked at me,
you enslaved me,
in grace entered me
and out of love melted my mind.[1]

1 Manikkavachakar, *Tiruvachakam*, Hymn 38, 7, in Yocum 1982, p. 142.

2 Confirmation of such a date comes from the lettering on the manuscript held in the saint's left hand, which is inscribed in Tamil characters of the twelfth century. See New Delhi 1983, p. 130.

These were the passionate words addressed to Shiva by saint Manikkavachakar, one-time minister to Varaguna Pandya of Madurai, who reigned during the second half of the ninth century. Hagiographic legend relates Manikkavachakar's conversion by Shiva himself, whom he encountered in the guise of a teacher while on his way to purchase horses for the Pandya cavalry. Manikkavachakar used the money instead to build a great temple to Shiva, for which he was twice imprisoned by King Varaguna before finally being permitted to leave the king's service and join his teacher.

Manikkavachakar wrote a large and varied body of poems, which constitute the *Tiruvachakam*, the eighth book of the Tamil sacred canon, and the esteem in which his verses are held is attested by his title, 'He whose words are rubies'. Shiva temples generally possess two images of Manikkavachakar, one being placed before the temple's image of Shiva as Nataraja (Lord of Dance). The second stands as part of the *nalvar* or 'Revered Four' poet-saints, alongside child saint Sambandar, saint Appar and saint Sundarar.

This smoothly modelled image portrays Manikkavachakar in characteristic mode, his right hand raised in a gesture of teaching and the left holding his typical attribute, a palm-leaf manuscript inscribed 'om nama shivaya' or 'praise be to Shiva'. He is shown with typical simplicity, wearing a short waist cloth and a sacred thread, with a simple neck chain and bangle. His face, calm and peaceful, has a gentle smile. The image is a fine piece from the middle Chola period, created around the year 1100.[2]

19   Saint Chandesha

c. 970
Bronze, H. 48 cm

The British Museum, London

One solid image of Chandesha, having two arms,
five *viral* and five *torai* in height from feet to hair;
one solid image of his father, having two arms,
represented as having fallen down and lying on the ground,
six *viral* and seven *torai* in length from feet to hair;
one solid image of Chandesha, having two arms,
receiving a boon, nine *viral* in length;
one flower garland given to him as a boon,
sixteen *viral* in length and half a *viral* in breadth, and two *torai* in thickness;
one solid aureola covering these images, two *muram* in circumference.[1]

1 *SII* 1916, inscription no. 29, p. 137. Edited by the author. The ancient measurement of *torai* ('rice grain') is equivalent to 18 mm, *viral* ('finger') to 1.44 cm and *muram* ('elbow to fingertips') to 34.56 cm.

According to this detailed inscription, a multi-piece bronze group celebrating the legend of Chandesha was commissioned for the great temple of Chola emperor Rajaraja (r. 985–1014) at Tanjavur. It appears that Rajaraja was deeply impressed by the story of this cowherd who attained sainthood through a single dramatic incident when he defended a Shiva *linga* – the pillar-like form representing the god. Legend speaks of the young boy worshipping a simple mud *linga* and using milk from the cows he tended for the ritual daily lustration. When his father came to chastise him for wasting the milk, Chandesha was so absorbed in meditation that he did not hear. His angry father kicked the *linga* and Chandesha lashed out with his staff, which miraculously turned into Shiva's sacred axe. Pleased by the intensity of Chandesha's devotion, Shiva and Uma blessed him with a divine garland.

During the Chola period, earlier simple shrines began to be converted into impressive stone temples and a supervising agent was needed to ensure the sanctity of the shrines. Chandesha became guardian of Shiva temples, and his bronze image was placed in a shrine within the temple grounds. Devotees still customarily stop before Chandesha's shrine, clapping to demonstrate that their hands are empty and that they are not carrying away any temple property.

This bronze Chandesha stands in relaxed contropposto, palms joined in adoration and hair piled high upon his head in imitation of Shiva's matted locks. In this and other images from the early Chola period, the battleaxe, now missing, was cast separately and placed in the crook of the arm; later the axe was cast of a piece with the sculpted figure.

3

Vishnu and His Imagery

That nectar-like Lord
whose sweetness never cloys,
that ambrosial Lord of Arangam,
with ever fresh garland of wild flowers
upon whose chest Lakshmi Devi sports,
They sing his praises,
mind intoxicated with love,
dancing and singing in wild joy,
lost to the world around
calling upon him repeatedly,
The eyes that feast upon
this crowd of devotees,
blessed indeed are those eyes![1]

THUS SANG VAISHNAVA saint Kulashekhara in a hymn dedicated to the beautiful lord Vishnu enshrined in the temple at Shrirangam. The hymn seems to have been a favourite of the Chola king Kulottunga I (r. 1070–1125), since an inscription dated 1088 speaks of a festival at which the monarch and god Vishnu sat in state and listened to the hymn to which the quoted verse belongs.[2]

Vishnu is the god who wears a long lower garment and a crown and sports on his chest a mole-like emblem called the *shrivatsa*. He favours the sacred basil leaf and wears a long wild-flower garland. In his two rear hands he holds his attributes: a discus – his weapon of choice – and a conch shell, whose sound is heard in all Vishnu temples. His right front hand invariably makes the gesture of benediction while his left hand typically rests elegantly on his hip. Vishnu is always found in bodily form within the sanctum of his temples; additional figures of Vishnu are sculpted in stone on temple walls and created from bronze. Vishnu's prime consort is Lakshmi, also known as Sri, goddess of wealth and fortune, from whom he is rarely separated. His second consort is the Earth Goddess or Bhu Devi, also known as Bhu Lakshmi, whom he rescued from drowning in cosmic waters.

It is believed that Vishnu is incarnated on earth whenever righteousness decreases and unlawful behaviour is on the rise. In the sacred text of the *Bhagavad Gita*, he explains:

To protect men of virtue
and destroy men who do evil,
to set the standard of sacred duty
I appear in age after age.[3]

The list of Vishnu's ten avatars varies slightly: an inscription dating from about 600 at Mamallapuram in Tamil Nadu lists them as Matsya (fish), Kurma (tortoise), Varaha (boar), Narasimha (man-lion), Vamana (dwarf), Parashurama, Rama, Krishna, Buddha and Kalki, the avatar that is yet to come. Theologians explain that there is no lessening of the godhead when Vishnu takes birth on earth. Vishnu himself is said to demonstrate this by plucking a single hair from his head to indicate that his essential essence is diminished by only one hair when he takes avatar.

The Vaishnava poet-saints of Tamil Nadu viewed Vishnu as manifesting himself in five ways, ranging from *para*, the highest form, seen only in heaven, through the avatars, to the *archa* or image of worship. They assigned an exceptionally elevated position to this image, which one scholar fittingly describes as 'a personal god, luminous and complete with all auspicious qualities; it is transcendent and supreme, yet easily accessible'.[4]

1 Kulashekhara, *Perumal Tirumoli*, 9.3, in Dehejia 1988, p. 94.
2 Dehejia 1988, p. 95. See also *SII* 1929, inscription no. 70, p. 51.
3 Miller 1986, p. 49.
4 Narayanan 1985, p. 54.

20 Vishnu

c.1100
Bronze, 84.7 × 35.6 cm

The National Museum, New Delhi

Eyes like red lotuses, lips like red fruit,
O four-shouldered one, ambrosia, my life,
Lord of Venkatam Hill
where glowing gems make night into day,
I, your servant, cannot bear
even for a second to be away
from your feet.[1]

1 Nammalvar, *Tiruvaymoli*, 6, 10.9,
in Narayanan 1994, p.171.

2 Kulashekhara, *Perumal Tirumoli*,
Hymn 4.9, in Dehejia 1988, p.92.

With these words the ninth-century Vaishnava saint Nammalvar sang of the beauty of
the image of Vishnu at Venkata (modern Tirupati), which remains today an exceedingly
sacred Vaishnava temple. The unknown artist of this Vishnu bronze, created around the
year 1100, some two centuries after the poem's composition, captured that same beauty
in smooth, flowing line and form. Vishnu stands firmly on both feet – contropposto
is never used for this god – holding his attributes of discus and conch shell in his two rear
hands. His front right hand is raised in the gesture of benediction, while the left hand
rests casually against his thigh. The image has the firm, grounded stability seen in Kaveri
Delta bronzes created during the reign of Kulottunga I (r. 1070–1125). Vishnu is richly
adorned with an entire range of jewelled ornaments and wears a tall cylindrical crown
from which escaping strands of hair rest along his shoulders. His long patterned waist
cloth, resting in pleats on either side of his limbs and between his legs, is arranged in
elaborately tied loops and folds and held by a girdle with a lion-head clasp.

The beauty of Vishnu was a recurring theme of sacred songs. Another ninth-
century saint, Kulashekhara, longed to be an inanimate object at Venkata if it would
give him the chance to gaze at Vishnu:

O Lord, O Venkata,
Would that I were a step
at the entrance to your shrine,
trodden upon by devotees,
by gods and apsaras [celestial nymphs]
who crowd to worship you –
…
ceaselessly I need to see
your lips of coral hue.
May I lie as a step
upon your threshold?[2]

21 Bhu Varaha Embracing Goddess Earth

Thirteenth century
Bronze, 45.5 × 30 cm

Victoria and Albert Museum, London

Once long ago
for the sake of the maiden earth
forlorn in moss-ridden body,
he took the shameful form
of a filthy
water-dripping boar.[1]

1 Andal, *Nacciyar Tirumoli*, Hymn 11.8, in Dehejia 1990B, p. 117.

2 Nammalvar, *Tiruvaymoli*, Hymn 10, 10.7, in Carman and Narayanan 1989, p. 255.

When the earth, personified as the goddess Bhu Devi, was in danger of drowning in the waters of the cosmic ocean, Vishnu took avatar as the giant boar Varaha and dived to the ocean's depths to rescue her. The verse quoted above, sung by the female saint Andal, focuses on the lowliness of the form that the great Vishnu took for the love of the Earth Goddess. By contrast, saint Nammalvar sang of the resplendent form of Vishnu as Varaha:

Like a blue mountain that clutches
and lifts up two crescent moons,
my Father, you, as a resplendent boar,
raised your tusks, carrying earth.[2]

Down the ages, monarchs in India described themselves as saviours of the earth and compared themselves to Vishnu in his Varaha avatar.

This bronze image of the late thirteenth century portrays Vishnu Varaha in human form with a striking boar head topped with a crown. He sits on a lotus seat in the *lalitasana* posture, with one leg folded and the other resting upon the hood of a five-headed cobra, denizen of the waters from which he has rescued the earth. The Earth Goddess is portrayed as a lovely young woman, richly adorned and wearing a breast band. She sits on his folded left knee with her palms joined in adoration while Varaha's two front arms gently enfold her. His rear hands hold his characteristic attributes of the discus and conch shell and his *shrivatsa* is portrayed as a triangle against his upper right shoulder. The bronze piece, with its flowing lines and tight composition, is a fine example of late Chola-period artistry.

22   Yoga Narasimha

c. 1250
Bronze, H. 55.2 cm

The Cleveland Museum of Art,
Gift of Dr Norman Zaworski,
1973.187

She danced and danced
with melting heart,
Sang song after song
eyes brimming with tears,
Searching everywhere
crying 'Narasingha!',
She wilts and fades
this maiden young.[1]

1 Nammalvar, *Tiruvaymoli*, Hymn 2,
4.1, in Dehejia 1988, p. 114.

2 *Padma Purana*, 5, 42,
in Soifer 1991, p. 191.

In an unusual verse composed by the poet-saint Nammalvar, a mother thus describes her daughter, who has fallen in love with the fierce lion-headed Narasimha.

Vishnu took avatar in the composite form of the man-lion Narasimha in order to destroy the evil king Hiranyakashipu, who had secured a boon from god Brahma that made him near invincible. Hiranyakashipu could not be killed by gods, demons, beasts or men; not during the day or the night; not indoors or outdoors; not on earth or in the heavens; and not through the use of any known weapon. Safeguarded thus, he forbade the worship of Vishnu and made life intolerable for his people. To destroy him without violating any of the boon's conditions, Vishnu took a form that was neither man, beast, god nor demon, tore him apart with his lion claws (not a conventional weapon) on the threshold of his palace (neither indoors nor outdoors), holding him in the air (neither earth nor heaven) at dusk (neither night nor day).

Narasimha is shown in the peaceable form that he assumes after his great feat of destruction, as described in the *Padma Purana*, a voluminous ancient sacred text that is a compendium of myth and legend and is thought to date to around the year 500:

You who are the most ancient supreme being, they call you the best body
and the supreme Brahma, the highest yoga and the most excellent speech,
the supreme mystery, and the highest path.[2]

A withdrawn Narasimha is seated with a yoga band around his legs, his two front hands resting against his knees in a position of quiet meditation, and his two rear hands displaying Vishnu's attributes of discus and conch shell (here missing).

23 Sita

c.980–90
Bronze, 66 × 20 cm

Linden-Museum, Stuttgart

As I follow behind you I shall no more tire on the path than on our pleasure beds…
The dust raised by heavy winds that will settle on me,
my love, I shall look upon as the costliest sandalwood cream…
The leaves and roots and fruit you gather with your own hands
and give to me, however much or little there is, will taste like nectar to me…
To be with you is heaven, to be without you is hell.[1]

1 Valmiki, *Ramayana*, Book 2: *Ayodhya*, Chapter 27, 10–20, in Pollock 2005, pp.177–9.

Down the centuries, Sita has been hailed as the ideal wife and a model for Indian womanhood. The story of Rama, prince of Ayodhya, and Sita is a very human story of a newly wed wife who insists on following her husband into exile, and a man who reproaches himself bitterly for having left his lovely wife alone and unguarded in the forest, leading to her abduction. According to the *Ramayana* (*Story of Rama*), generally believed to have been composed between 200 BCE and 200 CE, Rama retreated to the forest with his brother Lakshmana and Sita, who was there abducted by the demon king of Lanka, Ravana. Following an alliance with the monkey-general Hanuman, Rama crossed the sea to Lanka and fought a battle of colossal proportions to rescue Sita and slay Ravana. After Sita's long imprisonment and rescue, her story ends tragically with Rama's ultimate rejection in the face of suspicions raised by his subjects about her chastity. No hint of tragedy appears, however, in this, or indeed other bronze images of Sita. Rama was a man on earth, but he was also an avatar of god Vishnu, with Sita as his divine consort, and the bronzes emphasise the aspect of divinity.

This slender bronze, which captures Sita's youthful beauty and a flowing sense of movement, was created by a master artist towards the very end of the tenth century. Her rich adornment suggests not her life of exile in the forest but rather her return to Ayodhya as queen. A chest belt known as a *channavira* rests between her breasts and then separates to encircle her torso. Additional ornaments include a pendant high around the throat, a broad beaded necklace, heavy beaded bracelets, armlets and tasselled elbow bands. Her patterned skirt is held in place by a jewelled hip belt, from which beaded loops descend.

24　Monkey General Hanuman

c. 1020

Bronze, H. 41 cm

Victoria and Albert Museum, Bequest
of Lord Curzon

In leaping I shall make the mountains tremble, leaping monkeys.
And as I leap the sea, the force of my thighs will carry along the
blossoms of vines, shrubs and trees on every side.
They will follow behind me as I leap through the sky this very day,
so that my path will resemble the Milky Way in the heavens…
I shall scatter the clouds. I shall make the mountains tremble.
Intent upon my leaping, I shall stir up the sea.[1]

1 Valmiki, *Ramayana*, Book 4:
Kishkindha, Chapter 66, 15–20,
in Lefeber 2005, pp. 389–91.

2 A popular Sanskrit prayer
to Hanuman, known in both
north and south India.

3 According to the Victoria and Albert
Museum's records, this image is part
of the bequest of Lord Curzon,
viceroy of India 1899–1905, to whom
it was given by the residents of the
town of Coimbatore.

In the *Ramayana* (*Story of Rama*, 200 BCE–200 CE), Rama, heir to the throne of
Ayodhya and one of the avatars of Vishnu, was driven into exile with his wife, Sita,
and brother Lakshmana. When Sita was abducted by Ravana, demon king of Lanka,
Rama enlisted the help of the monkey-general Hanuman.

Humble, yet powerful, the monkey Hanuman is adored by countless devotees
for the impossible feat he performed of jumping across the ocean to Lanka, giving Sita
a message from Rama, and returning to prepare for the final battle. Devotees address
him in a variety of contexts, beseeching him to help them achieve their individual tasks:

Lord who achieved the impossible
with you how can one speak of the impossible?
Messenger of Rama, Ocean of mercy
make my task achievable, O Lord.[2]

Vishnu temples normally house a foursome group of bronzes to represent the legend:
Rama, Sita, Lakshmana and Hanuman.

Except for his long tail, this bronze Hanuman is more human than simian,
bending forward slightly with his hand in front of his mouth in his typical gesture
of humility. He is richly adorned and his short, patterned waist cloth, tied in
elaborate knots on both sides, is held in place with a hip belt with a large floral
clasp. This whimsical bronze from the western Kongu region of Tamil Nadu is
a creation of early eleventh-century date.[3]

25 Krishna Dancing on Kaliya

Eleventh century
Bronze, H.87.6 cm

Asia Society, New York,
Collection of Mr and Mrs
John D. Rockefeller 3rd, 1979.22

They trembled
the *gopis* and *gopas*.
He climbed upon
the flowering blue *katampa* oak,
he dived into the waters,
danced on captive Kaliya.[1]

1 Andal, *Nacciyar Tirumoli*, Hymn 4.4,
in Dehejia 1990B, p.87.

A favourite among the many heroic feats that Krishna performed as a youth was his subduing of the aquatic serpent demon Kaliya who, together with his serpent queens, lived in the waters of the River Yamuna near Mathura, south of Delhi, and terrorised the inhabitants of the region. Climbing upon a tall oak on the river bank, Krishna dived into the deep waters where he battled with and overcame Kaliya. Acquiescing to the entreaties of Kaliya's distraught serpent wives, he refrained from killing him, obtaining a promise that Kaliya would change his ways and leave the waters of the Yamuna. Krishna then danced a triumphant dance upon Kaliya's serpent hood.

The artist of this magnificent bronze has cast Krishna not as a humble cowherd but in the role of a young, richly adorned prince with a crown-like headdress. With his left leg placed at an angle on the serpent's hood and the other gracefully poised, Krishna dances elegantly upon recumbent Kaliya, who is portrayed with a human torso and serpentine lower body, lying submissively with his hands joined in the *anjali* gesture of adoration. With one hand triumphant Krishna holds aloft the serpent's tail, while the other makes a gesture of protection and benediction. This evocative bronze, poised in equilibrium, conveys a sense of dynamic movement and is the work of a master artist of the eleventh century.

26   Krishna, with Consorts Rukmini and Satyabhama and Divine Eagle Garuda

Thirteenth century
Bronze,
68.9 × 24.8 cm,
87 × 40.6 cm,
71.8 × 23.5 cm,
49.8 × 22.9 cm

Los Angeles County Museum of Art,
Gift of Mr and Mrs Hal B. Wallis

It's incredible – you were born! You grew up!
You showed your strength at the great battle of Bharat!
You showed your valour to the five brothers!
     The wonder of all this!
You enter my soul, stand within it, melt it, and eat it.
O radiant flame of the sky! When can I reach you?[1]

1 Nammalvar, *Tiruvaymoli*, 5, 10.1,
   in Carman and Narayanan
   1989, p. 166.

This majestic grouping of god Krishna flanked by his two queens relates to the final phase of his life on earth, when he ruled as king of Dvarka in western India. While his exploits as a youthful cowherd undoubtedly entranced devotees, Krishna's post-cowherd life on earth was, in some ways, of deeper significance. It was during this later phase that he played the role of charioteer to Arjuna in the Mahabharata war, referred to in the quoted verse, and explicated the philosophy of the *Bhagavad Gita*. He is often referred to in this phase as 'Rajamannar' – 'He who Resembles a King'. The piece lays emphasis on Krishna's aspect as avatar of Vishnu through the presence of Vishnu's mount, the divine eagle Garuda, who is usually seen only with Vishnu himself.

Beautiful Krishna stands regally poised in elegant contropposto, his right hand lowered to hold a staff and the left elbow raised to rest upon the shoulder of his second consort, Satyabhama. His pose closely resembles images of Shiva as Vrishabhavana (Rider of the Bull), in which Shiva stands with his arm similarly poised to rest on the bull Nandi (see cat. 13). The assured rendering of this richly adorned image is remarkable and the imposing bronze appears to belong to around the year 1200.

The artist who created Krishna also modelled the image of his senior queen, Rukmini, who stands to Krishna's proper right. Daughter of the king of Kundinapura, Rukmini was rescued by Krishna before the eyes of the guests assembled for her forced wedding to the Chedi prince Sisupala. With a lotus in her left hand and her right hand resting downwards, Rukmini wears a long skirt of patterned fabric and a breast band across her bosom, a feature that emphasises her identification with Vishnu's chief consort, Sri Lakshmi, who also wears a breast band. The image is an accomplished bronze of fluid modelling that emphasises beauty of line and form.

Krishna's junior queen, Satyabhama, was daughter of King Shatrajit, who gave her in marriage to Krishna in appreciation for Krishna's recovery of his stolen miraculous gem, the Shyamantaka, which dispelled darkness. Satyabhama was regarded by devotees as an incarnation of Vishnu's second consort, Bhu Lakshmi. Richly adorned, Satyabhama, with her hair piled on her head in a similar manner to Krishna's, stands poised to his proper left and would have held a blue lotus in her right hand. The less supple modelling of Satyabhama's figure, however, and such details as her high, rounded breasts placed close together and the circles incised around her nipples, suggest that two different artists were responsible for the crafting of the images of the two queens.

It seems likely that this second artist was also responsible for carving Garuda, Vishnu's soaring divine eagle mount, who outpaces the wind in flight. His firm, arresting figure is portrayed in human form but with a beaked nose, fangs and wings, as he stands with palms joined in adoration of his master.

This remarkably refined group seems, then, to have been the creation of two different artists, one especially gifted at rendering movement, both working around the year 1200.

27 Krishna Rajamannar

Twelfth century
Bronze, H. 101.5 cm

Mr D. A. Latchford Collection

Do they smell of camphor
or of the lotus bloom?
Do they taste sweet
his sacred lips of coral hue?
O white conch from the fathomless sea,
I long to know,
tell me the taste, the fragrance
of the lips of Madhavan
who broke the elephant's tusk.[1]

1 Nacchiyar Tirumoli, Hymn 7, 1,
in Dehejia 1990B, p.99.
2 Nacchiyar Tirumoli, Hymn 11, 9,
in Dehejia 1990B, p.117.

The conch shell is one of Vishnu's key attributes, which he sounds like a trumpet.
Deeply in love with the god, the female poet-saint Andal, writing around the year
800, imagines herself as his bride and addresses an entire hymn to the fortunate
conch so intimately close to her lord. She pictures Vishnu in his avatar as Krishna,
referring to him as Madhavan, one of his alternate names.

In this exquisite portrayal Krishna is shown as the majestic Rajamannar
('He who Resembles a King'), as indicated by his raised hand. He stands gracefully
poised in an exaggerated *tribhanga* pose. This is the same lord seen in cat. 26, flanked
on his right by queen Rukmini and on his left by his second queen, Satyabhama.
In another hymn, Andal makes specific reference to the 'divine bridegroom' who
intervened and snatched away Rukmini at her forced wedding to prince Sisupala.

All was set for the wedding –
Sisupala was resolved
to take her hand in marriage.
All of a sudden his glow vanished,
he stood petrified.
The divine bridegroom stepped in,
took her hand in marriage…[2]

The elegant bronze embodies the sophistication and artistic mastery of the late
Chola period and echoes the technical virtuosity seen in the foursome group.

4

The Jain Faith

Jainism was formulated during the fifth century BCE by Mahavira, chieftain of the republic of Vaishali in eastern India. Mahavira left home at around the age of thirty and, upon achieving enlightenment, became known as the Jina – 'Victor'. Emphasising penance and austerity, the faith developed and Mahavira was seen as the last in a line of twenty-four Jinas.

Jainism acquired early popularity in south India, where a number of small caverns were occupied by Jain ascetics and carry Tamil inscriptions dating from the second century BCE to the third century CE. Although the Jains originally coexisted happily with Hindus, a rivalry developed towards the end of the fifth century. The Jain faith continued to attract a devout group of worshippers, however, and, throughout the Chola period, royalty extended them support. For instance, Kundavai, the sister of emperor Rajaraja Chola (r. 985–1014), constructed one Shiva temple, one Vishnu temple and two Jain temples.[1]

The sensuous modelling, fluid outlines and decorative flair of the various Jain bronzes, and indeed those of Buddhist affiliation, indicate that the same sculpture workshops produced bronze images for Hindu, Buddhist and Jain temples.

1 Venkataraman 1976, pp.72–84

28 Jina, probably Mahavira

Tenth century
Bronze, 74.3 × 35.6 cm

Private collection

Lord, you are a silver coin among planets,
Shining with a thousand victorious rays…
Lord, you are grand from your toes to your head.
Drums resound in the firmament.
Lord, your knees are like a welcome rain,
Like a five-coloured fruit from a wish-granting cow.[1]

1 Kshamavijay, quoted in Cort 2001, p.203.

This aesthetically satisfying Jina image is a paradox, portraying the detached saviour of the world performing penance, but at the same time incorporating that touch of sensuousness characteristic of Chola workmanship. While each of the twenty-four Jinas has his own attribute, these are frequently missing, as in this image, which probably represents Mahavira. All images of Jinas show the figure standing in *kayotsarga* – a position of yogic detachment with hands stretched firmly down at the sides, representing an impassive posture of penance.

The image is starkly plain except for a waistband. The sensitive modelling of the smooth outlines of the body, the rounded buttocks, and the strong yet soft thighs, all speak of Chola workmanship. The accentuation of the knees calls to mind the words quoted above from a hymn written by a Jain monk in the year 1735. A highly accomplished work of the early Chola period, the bronze is set into a lotus pedestal with lugs, confirming that, like Hindu bronzes, it was a portable festival image.

Appendix A
The Vikramacholanula: A Chola Processional Poem

DAUD ALI

Though both secular and religious processions were well established throughout the Indian subcontinent by early medieval times, such promenades saw greater ritual elaboration and literary commemoration in south India during the Chola period (c.950–1250). This is perhaps demonstrated most clearly by the emergence of a new genre of literature known as *ula* – a Tamil word that referred to both a procession and a poem describing it. The earliest *ula* poem, which describes Shiva's procession around Mount Kailasa, dates from the ninth century. The genre was considerably expanded by the celebrated poet Ottakuttar, who gained the title 'emperor among poets' for his service at the courts of no less than three Chola kings in the twelfth century. He composed a trilogy of *ula*s known as the *Muvarula* praising each of these kings. The extracts presented below were dedicated to the king Vikrama Chola (r.1118–35), who was famous for his extensive renovations at the holy shrine of Shiva at Chidambaram. The following years saw the composition of many *ula*s, with some seventy surviving today, dedicated variously to gods, kings and men of virtue. Scholars have long noted a symmetry between the symbology and rituals of gods in south India and those of kings. Medieval texts do not draw sharp distinctions between the royal and the divine and tend to see them both within a larger hierarchy of cosmic lordship. Though preserved in manuscript form, the *ula* poems were recited aloud at court or in temples and seem to have been accompanied by music.

The *ula* genre begins by praising the poem's protagonist (who was sometimes also its patron), describing in detail his daily routine and departure on procession. It then depicts crowds of lovelorn women thronging the streets and balconies to see the protagonist move through the city. In the case of royal *ula*s, these were women who seem to have been largely of high birth, acquired through capture and tribute during war and housed by the king along the 'Royal Street' of the capital city, Tanjavur. They bear great similarity to the women who were bound to the gods of temples, the famous *devadasi*, who were housed in streets surrounding the temple. These women are likely to have been the female onlookers in religious *ula*s. Both palace and temple women often appear as pious donors in temple inscriptions from the Chola period. The *ula* divides them into seven different age groups: *petai* (ages five to eight), *petumpai* (ages eight to eleven), *mankai* (ages twelve to thirteen), *matantai* (ages fourteen to nineteen), *arivai* (ages twenty to twenty-five), *terivai* (ages twenty-six to thirty-one) and *perilampen* (ages thirty-two to forty). The social significance of these divisions, which apparently mark stages of sexual maturity, is far from clear, but they seem to derive from courtly traditions depicting the stages of erotic love. At one level, the vivid descriptions of these women celebrate their beauty as a mark of the power and majesty of the poem's protagonist. At another level they seem to have served as literary devices to explore the emotions of loyalty and devotion that structured the wider world of religious and secular affiliation in medieval Tamil society.

The excerpts from the *Vikramacholanula* presented below are intended to convey a flavour of the genre and the cultural world that surrounded processions in medieval south India both lordly and divine.

ONE DAY THE KING, who was living in the eyes of lotus-seated goddess Lakshmi, adorned with some of the pearls given to him as tribute by the Pandya king, smeared with sandalwood paste from the Pandya's mountain, with a sounding anklet on his feet, which were stroked by the sweet southern breeze from the Pandya's land,[1] arose from sweet sleep on his long, moon-like bed, under a canopy of pearls, where he had enjoyed the night with the empress known as the 'Goddess of the Seven Worlds'. Her hair was scattered with blossoms, breasts large, eyelids black with collyrium, shoulders garlanded with clusters of blossoms. She was like a joyful swan, and was served by a retinue of women with warring, sword-like eyes…The king bathed in the beauteous Kaveri River and put on a bracelet made from fresh tender sprouts of Aruku grass from the hand of his priests. He then worshipped that light of the *Vedas*, the flame of the silver mountain, Shiva, with a crescent moon in his hair, a darkened throat, a refreshing and ruddy ethereal form – the sole luminary of the gods, the sweet three-eyed one. Having dispersed gifts, the king called for his ornaments, of the most excellent pre-eminence, for his decoration. On his face, which was like a bloomed flower around which bees thronged, where the Goddess of Eloquence resided, glittered *makara* earrings.[2] On his shoulders, where the broad-breasted Goddess of the Earth stayed, were epaulets brilliant with gems. On his hand, where the unsteady Goddess of Fame was fixed, sparkled a bracelet of gems. On his chest, where the Goddess of Fortune lovingly embraced him, shone with increasing splendour a jewel from the sea. On his hip, where the beautiful Goddess of Victory, now at peace, resided, was a beautiful sword. Having put on these numerous rare ornaments of suitably lofty beauty, he obtained matchless elegance and grace such that it seemed as if Shiva had bestowed on him, while he was bowing with the crest of his crown, the beauty Shiva had once attained as 'respect' from Kamadeva's bow.[3] The king then departed the palace, where a beautiful male elephant stood before him…The reach of that elephant's trunk, when agitated and extended during battle, is difficult to escape. When his deadly tusks are heated in anger they can puncture, break and scorch even

mountain peaks. He tramples the lands of other kings who have been laid low and disgraced and, boiling with rage, dispatches their souls above in battle. The king climbed, step by step, upon that standing Airavata, who supplies souls to Yama, the God of Death, and sat.[4] The shade from his great parasol, fit for his eminence, cooled him, while two *chauris* of tufted hair fanned him with gentle gusts of cool air.[5] A single conch shell sounded, and then a multitude joined in, all sounding together, while the tabor drums roared.

HIS RETINUE

Swordsmen, who had left their homelands and were feared by men, crowded together and the great and powerful banner of the tiger rose above them all. The king was attended by the Tontaiman,[6] who was bestowed a *parani*[7] when in a single day's battle he scattered the armies of Malainadu and defeated the distant Tennar, Maluvar, Sinhala and king of sweet Kudaka…; the Brahman named Kannan, from Kanjam, with its high walls touching the clouds, who was a brilliant minister and daily oversaw the king's servants, the armour on the king's shoulders and the sword for terrible wars; the Bana king, who, holding a drawn bow in his hand in battle, sent the souls of enemy kings to Yama, and their rotting bodies to be consumed by ghosts, while he himself obtained the earrings of the ladies who had provided their food…; the king of the Senji, with solid fortifications and beautiful ruddy ramparts…; Vattavan, whose great elephants pounded and destroyed the three walls of the enemy city of Manyakheta in a great battle; the warrior from the beautiful land of Ceti, who ruined the fort of the Karnatas and slayed the headless bodies that rose up [from the battlefield]…; Adikan, who cut to pieces the elephant of northern Kalinga and defeated the great king of Ottiya; Vallavan, the Nolamban, who, on a completely mad rutting elephant, received under his parasol the Pandya's Kottaru and Kollam;[8] Tikattan of the red-trunked elephant, who trampled Kutaku mountain and bewildered the kingdom of Kongu, protected by its elevation; and finally the capable rulers of Anga, Kosala, Malwa and Magadha, as well as the Villavan and Keralan, Pandya and Pallava kings. This great

crowd of rival kings and feudatories collected before him and on his flanks.

THE CROWDS OF WOMEN ENTER THE STREET

Like a flock of swans on the sandbanks of the seashore's groves, like lightning flashes in the clouds, like a multitude of waves following upon one another, like a flock of mountain peacocks, the women appear suddenly everywhere on the street, their moon-like foreheads sweating, their eyes afire, glancing around and showing their feelings openly. They crowd together with ornaments of brilliantly shining jewels and rows of bright-burning diamonds. Coming with bowing heads, having breasts like pots full of ambrosia, adorned with pearls that glitter and shine, they stay in groups, their cruel gazes shooting poison and their crimson mouths and sharp teeth making idle banter. They gather like celestial singers on the floors of the crystal white palace in the heavens, playing with their fingers the *vina*, *yal*,[9] pipe and strap drum, keeping the beat with their feet. Their eyes, blackened with collyrium, gaze without blinking; their flower feet do not touch the earth; their fragrant garlands stay fresh and unwithered; collecting on the moon balconies of unfading beauty, they are like incomparable divine dancing girls in their speech, form, radiance and feeling.

PETAI

…The big eyes of this tender young girl who still has not left the side of her mother, are innocent and like small drops of honey. The deer, the peacock, the green parrot, the cuckoo and the swan follow her affectionately, as if they were her toys… Cool pearls from Korkai, used as rice in play cooking, are in her hands. The other girls enter the streets, which are full of golden creepers, and play at their edges…Without fixating on his flower face, adorned with a *tilaka*…without hankering after his beautiful chest, so suitable [for embrace], without moving towards his flawless flower hands, without regarding his lotus feet, without dwelling on the great brilliance of his graceful body, the eyes and hearts of this girl becomes attracted to the cluster of red water lilies fixed upon his flower garland. Her heart melting, she cries 'Come, Mother! Get that garland for me.' Her mother replies with honeyed words, 'Oh! Do not fear that great one, who is nectar to women. We will go and ask him to give us that beautiful garland, but it will be very difficult to get it.' Tears splash down on her breasts, as she experiences the desire of the elder girls. She completely forgets the game of doling and serving sand-rice to the younger girls sitting with her.

PETUMPAI

Having left her childish prattle to her parrot, she now takes on the melodiousness of the hunter's flute [in her voice]…Her shy gaze she has devoted to her pet deer, and her eyes have now become spears daubed in poison. She has surrendered the tenderness of her body, brilliant to behold, to her *matavi* plant,[10] and now resembles a flash of lightning in the clouds…Having at one time the gentle gait of an approaching female swan, she now moves like a young virgin she elephant. The hair on her head is tied by pearls banded together by coral vines inlaid with clusters of brilliant gold…While [girls] with their companions run about in the street, come to the porches of their rumbling cloud palaces, adorned with all manner of charms, like the shapely carp-eyed goddess [Tirumakal][11] appearing like lightning, the eyes of the beautiful girl are locked on the warrior…Not removing her folded hands from worship, knowing no way of recovering her heart, which has been totally overwhelmed, bewildered by desire previously unknown to her, hair untied and dishevelled, flower garland loosened, she stands alone, while that hero among the Sembiyars,[12] served by the Pandya [king] and the Chera with his terrible spear, disappears down the street. The flying arrows aimed at these girls, suitable but not quite ready [for love] – are repulsed, falling to the ground. Kamadeva moves on.[13]

MANKAI

…The love kept in the *petumpai's* heart in her youth when she saw in her dreams our king, the emperor, born by the grace of God, has come to an end. She sets in her heart, to end her swooning, his image, beginning with his red lotus feet all the way up to his pure gold crown. During the day she sees him in the picture drawn by her hand; at night her dreams show that very image, and she is interested in nothing

else. 'The king, Jayatunga,[14] wearing a flower garland thick with nectar, riding on his war elephant, is coming down the street,' she says. 'All of you, give me your ornaments,' and, receiving them, she decorates herself. She drapes herself with a blossoming flower garland, wears a beautiful dress embroidered with fine gold, smears herself with sandalwood paste and puts on great jewels…Seeing this king on his passing war elephant, her mind and soul experience limitless joy.

MATANTAI

The *matantai* speaks sweetly as she embraces the heavy shoulder of her friend, and they ascend to the moon porch.[15] 'You tender vines! Let us divide equally and, watched by the happy dancers, play ball. If I am defeated, you will keep my garland. Otherwise, you have to get our king's garland and give it to me,' said the one who is like lightning, rolling her hair and tying tightly her breast band, and keeping in her hand a bunch of balls…Seeing the king's approach down the royal avenue, she forgets their wager and, not guarding her bracelets and fastened girdles, approaches bowing, swooning, trembling, fainting and weeping in loneliness. Her flawlessly preserved garment and beautiful girdle, inlaid with gold, slip down…and she faints onto the shoulder of the girl next to her. Kamadeva angrily steals her spirit in combat,[16] while her matrons, offering wise but vain advice, standing all around, afraid, mix rosewater and sandalwood and smear it on her body, and then pour drops of water upon her. They fan her, place her in moonlight, and bring the young south breeze, but it burns her. Will they not stop? But still they gather water lilies. Like a flood that spreads to low ground, her life and soul follow after the king along the noisy street while the girl trembles and perishes.

ARIVAI

Among women, she is like the nectar yielded from the ocean. Bees encircle the flower ties in her hair, which emit a honey scent. She has become a different girl…At this time, without any concern for the birds living in her care – the singing mynah, dancing peacock, flocks of young parrots and young swans – she goes off and enters the *kurava* tree bower, covered with abundant

blossoms, in her lovely young flower garden. 'Oh swan,' she laments, 'daily you play in the Kaveri, belonging to the family of that king on his strong elephant. Oh heron, you live in the great [port city of] Poompukar in the Chola kingdom,' she swoons. 'Dark cuckoo, you sing from the gardens in the Chola's land,' she trembles. 'Peacock, with your magnificent feathers, you proudly reside in the Kolli hills and Neri mountain,' she pines. 'Bees, you live hovering continually on the great Aram garland of the Chola, with its cool flower buds,' she cries in desperation…As she was standing like this she heard the sound of the conchs that herald the capable Akalanka,[17] king among kings, who like lightning was gone. Because of overwhelming desire, her unwavering timidity and well-guarded simplicity were suddenly lost. When she saw the Chola her lotus face bloomed as if opened by the rays of the sun…This girl, unlike others, has obtained the power to have a claim on the beautiful flower garland[18] of that lord of the ever-flowing Kaveri.

TERIVAI

She is like unadulterated sugar-cane juice, like an unwithering golden branch whose flower buds bear sprouts ripe for the picking…like a ruby that is maddeningly not for sale, like nectar that can be enjoyed tirelessly by everyone. At twilight, the south breeze comes from the well-kept garden like a messenger into the jewelled palace. Her affectionate companions smear sandalwood paste on her and the fragrance of it diffuses; jasmine thronged by spotted bees emits its bouquet…She listens to the lute player and his songstress, lamenting all night until dawn, when the elephant with its headdress arrives, on which sits the lord of the earth surrounded by oceans and mountains, who is honoured and praised by many. She quickly recovers her spirit, which had been unable to bear the agitation caused by the lute's music…and stands before the elephant imploring him, 'Oh Airavata, you are like soul, body and feeling for me, are you not? Do not move from here!'

PERILAMPEN

This woman, keeping a jewel on her forehead, is different, with a full thigh that kills, like the trunk of a great elephant

belonging to the strong-shouldered Chola,
king of [the port city of] Korkai…Having
put on several fragrant garlands, applied
musk and adorned herself with ocean
pearls, she sits with her younger companion
in the beautiful flower garden…Her
companion pours the toddy into separate
cups and removes bees and froth from the
liquor…Taking a sip, she collapses onto
her companion, intoxicated, dreaming
pleasantly that the king has arrived and
embraced her with desire…but she awakes
suddenly…Seeing the approach of the fierce
male elephant that carries Jayatunga,[19]
shaded by his umbrella of expanded lotuses,
the sweet-speeched one says 'I have been
tricked by the liquor into thinking my visions
were real.' She regains her composure and
folds her hands in reverence, but the next
moment an unquenchable infatuation
overtakes her again. She collapses onto
the shoulder of her companion, who runs
before the lofty royal elephant, saying
'Oh supreme king with the wheel,[20] ruler
of Vanji, Poompukar with its many palaces,
Madurai, Kanchi, and Uraiyur!…The many
jewels of your earth; the pearls sprung of the
waters of your seas, the diamonds from your
Neri mountain, the beautiful silks abounding
in your land – all these you have taken. But
the plumpness and heaviness of her breasts,
the strength of her cool thighs, her fresh
young complexion and her sleep – is seizing
these also in accordance with the *dharma*[21]
followed by your ancient family?'…Saying
this, her companion saluted him; but
Kamadeva then bent his bow towards
this girl, as the munificent Chola, atop
his elephant…passed by in procession.

Notes

1 The pearls, the famous southern breeze, thought to be cooling, and the sandalwood paste, also a cooling agent, all come from the Pandya kingdom, which lay to the south and was a traditional rival to the Cholas.

2 The *makara* is a mythical beast similar to a crocodile and said to be the traditional mount of Kamadeva, god of love.

3 Kamadeva, the god of love (a cupid-like figure with a sugar-cane bow and flower arrows, known for his physical beauty) tried to distract Shiva with his charms while he was meditating. Shiva famously burned away Kamadeva's body with the meditative heat of a stern glance from his third eye, giving rise to the epithet 'bodiless' ('ananga') for Kamadeva. The conceit here is that by his piety in worshipping Shiva, the king has gained the unparalleled beauty that is proper to Kamadeva, which had in effect been taken as 'tribute' by Shiva.

4 Airavata was the name of the Hindu god Indra's elephant, the most famous elephant in the cosmos, and the Chola king's elephant was consequently called the same. Yama, god of death, ate men, and Airavata dispatched men to Yama and was hence his 'feeder'.

5 The parasol was a symbol of imperial majesty. *Chauris* are yak-tail fans.

6 Tontaiman is a king, like all those in the list that follows.

7 A poem traditionally composed in celebration of the slaying of a large number of enemy elephants.

8 The Nolamba king conquered the forts of Kottaru and Kollam, which belonged to the Pandya.

9 The *vina* is an Indian lute. The *yal* is another stringed instrument particular to south India.

10 The *matavi* is a type of tender creeper.

11 Tirumakal is the goddess of wealth and prosperity, also known as Lakshmi, consort of Vishnu.

12 Another name for the Cholas.

13 The text suggests that Kamadeva, god of love, accompanies the king and shoots arrows of love at the waiting women as he moves in the procession.

14 Another name for King Vikrama Chola.

15 'Moon porch' refers to open porches on the tall palaces, where women would go to spend time in the moonlight.

16 Because Kamadeva, like Cupid, makes lovers desire one another by attacking them with his arrows, he is often given martial qualities by poets.

17 Another of King Vikrama Chola's titles.

18 The flower garland signifies favour.

19 Another of King Vikrama Chola's titles.

20 Like the conch and parasol, the wheel is another symbol of kingship, implying universal rulership.

21 Traditions.

The Dance of Shiva
AUGUSTE RODIN

The sculptor Auguste Rodin (1840–1917) wrote this descriptive piece in 1913. He based it on a series of images taken in India in 1911 by an unidentified photographer. It is possible that the photographs are the work of Victor Goloubew, a wealthy Russian aristocrat and a member of the École Française d'Extrême Orient. An active archaeologist, Goloubew founded *Ars Asiatica* (1914–35), a journal dedicated to the art and architecture of the East, and established the internationally significant Archives Photographiques at the Musée Guimet in 1920.

Rodin came to write the piece through his friendship with Goloubew. His text was published in 1921 in the third edition of *Ars Asiatica*, where it was illustrated with twelve black-and-white heliotype plates by Léon Marotte. In all, six images each of two eleventh-century Chola bronze representations of Shiva Nataraja, one from Tiruvalangadu and one from Velankanni, were included. Both works form part of the extremely important collection of Chola bronzes housed at the Government Museum, Chennai.[1]

For his part, Rodin produced a portrait bust of Goloubew's wife, Nathalie, which was exhibited at the Salon d'Automne in Paris in 1905.[2] The photographs were deposited at the Musée National des Arts Asiatiques-Guimet, Paris, although they now belong to the Musée Rodin, Paris.

Adrian Locke

1 Their accession numbers are 236 and 234 respectively.
2 Grunfeld 1988, pp. 498–9n.

Victor Goloubew (?),
Detail of Shiva Nataraja from Velankanni, 1911.
Photograph. Musée Rodin, Paris/Meudon, Ph. 16465

ON LOOKING AT THE SHIVA GROUP AS A WHOLE

Full-blown in life, in the stream of life, air, sun, the feeling of being alive is overwhelming. This is the way the art of the Far East appears to us!

The divinity of the human form was obtained at that time, not because mankind was closer to its origins then, since our bodily form has remained exactly the same; but the servitude of today makes us believe we can liberate ourselves totally; and we are like fish out of water. There is a lack of taste.

From a certain angle, Shiva is a narrow crescent shape.

What a talent to take pride in one's body!

Today, beauty in bronze is immutable. The imperceptible movement of light. You can feel the motionless muscles, tensed together, ready to surge forward if the light changes position.

The shadow gets closer and closer, working its way over the masterpiece, giving it charm: the deep softness that comes from the darkness, that place where it lingers so long.

These hints of modelling! The fog of the body! Like something divinely ordered, there is no hint of revolt in this form: everything is in its place. We understand the rotation of the arm even when it is motionless by looking at the shoulder blade, the way it protrudes, the ribcage, the admirable way the ribs are attached, fixed by scalloped edgings to maintain the shoulder blade and its action in place. And the flank that continues this torso, constrained here, gripped there, then widening out to articulate the two thighs, two connectors, two levers, perfectly angled, delicate legs that disport themselves on the ground.

Victor Goloubew (?),
*Shiva Nataraja from
Velankanni,* 1911.
Photograph. Musée Rodin,
Paris/Meudon, Ph. 16464

IN FRONT OF A PROFILE OF SHIVA

The two hands separating the chest and the stomach are admirable. The gesture is graceful enough to compete with the Medici Venus, shielding her charms with her arm, as Shiva seems to protect himself with his ingenious gesture. The right-hand shadow divides the torso into two halves and slips down along the thighs; one of these is half in shadow, the other in chiaroscuro, in transferred shade. The pubis cannot be seen; it is hidden by the darkness.

To sum up, only the virtues of depth, opposition, lightness and power are worthwhile; not those details that are good only for themselves, useless flourishes that have no meaning in relation to movement.

These legs with their stretched muscles contain only strength.

These closed thighs, a double caress, jealously guarding their dark secret; the beautiful surface shadow is emphasised by the light of the thighs.

FACING SHIVA, FROM THE FRONT

According to artists, the pose is familiar; yet it has nothing banal about it; because in every pose nature intervenes so much! Above all, there are things that other people do not see: unknown depths, the wellsprings of life. There is grace in elegance; above grace, there is modelling; everything is exaggerated; we call it soft but it is most powerfully soft! Words fail me then.

Garlands of shadows stand out from the shoulder to the hip – from the jutting hip to the squared-off thigh.

FROM ANOTHER SIDE OF SHIVA

These two legs with different lighting; this thigh, transferring the shadow to the other leg.

If there were no inner modelling, the contour would not be plump and supple; it would be gaunt with that straight shadow.

ON THE SUPPOSEDLY PRIMITIVE ART OF SHIVA

Ignorant mankind simplifies and looks very crudely, removing life from a superior art in order to love the inferior, paying attention to nothing. You have to study more if you want to be absorbed and to see.

ON STUDYING SHIVA'S HEAD AT LENGTH

This swollen, prominent mouth, with its wealth of sensual expressions.

The tenderness of the mouth and of the eye are in harmony.

Like a well of pleasure the lips are surmounted by the wonderfully noble, palpitating nostrils.

The mouth, with its damp delights, undulates as sinuously as a snake: the eyes are shut, rounded, closed by a seam of eyelashes.

On this busy surface, the wings of the nose stand out tenderly.

The lips form words, moving when they escape. Such a delicious moving snake!

The eyes have only a corner in which to hide; the purity of line and the tranquillity of concealed stars.

The tranquil temple of these eyes; the tranquil drawing; the tranquil joy of this calm.

Everything stops at the chin, where all the curves converge.

The expression terminates and turns back on itself. The movements of the mouth disappear into the cheeks.

The curve from the ear echoes a small curve that pulls up the mouth, and also echoes, slightly, the wings of the nose; it forms a circle that passes under the nose and chin as far as the cheekbones.

The high curving cheekbones.

STILL FACING SHIVA'S ELOQUENT HEAD

This eye stays in the same place with its companion; auspiciously sheltered, it is voluptuous and luminous.

The closed eyes are like the sweetness of times gone by.

Those clearly drawn eyes, like a precious enamel.

The eyes in the casket of the eyelids: the arch of the eyebrows; the curve of the sinuous lips.

The mouth, home of the gentlest thoughts, but a volcano for fury.

The soul can be imprisoned in this bronze in material form captured for several centuries; longing for eternity on this mouth; the eyes that will see and speak.

Life enters and exits by the mouth, for ever, as bees go endlessly in and out; gentle scented breath.

This charming lost profile possesses the profile, but the profile in which the expression terminates, sinks down, leaving the beauty of the descending cheeks, which are joined to the sinews of the neck.

Glossary
of Terms

JOHN GUY

abhaya-mudra
gesture of fearlessness, reassurance
and protection offered by deity to
devotee, with right hand displayed
palm outwards and fingers raised.

abhiseka
'ritual bathing' – ceremonial
lustration of a sacred image with
water, milk, honey, curds and so on,
also performed to confer or confirm
kingship and marriage.

acharya
'observing the rules of his order'
– spiritual guide or teacher who
instructs students, especially
in the *Vedas*.

alamkara
ornament and embellishment,
without which images are seen
as incomplete.

alvar
'immersed [in god]' – south Indian
Vaishnava poet-saints, active
between sixth and tenth centuries;
their images are worshipped in
temples and processions.

ananda tandava
'dance of bliss' – associated
with south Indian representations
of Shiva Nataraja, especially
processional bronze images.

Andhaka
demon of darkness who was
blind but believed he had sight;
embodiment of spiritual blindness,
sometimes identified as wayward
son of Shiva, slain by Shiva with
his trident.

anjali-mudra
'two handfuls' – pose with
hands clasped together in
respectful greeting and adoration,
characteristic of subordinate deities,
attendant gods and devotees.

Appar
seventh-century Shaivite poet-saint,
one of the *muvar* ('Revered Three').

apsara
semi-divine female beings inhabiting
Hindu god Indra's paradise as
dancers and musicians, partnered
with *gandharas* – celestial musicians.

archa
cult image in sanctum of a temple.

avahana
invocation of a deity to inhabit
an icon, part of the opening
ritual of every *puja*.

avatar
'descent' – physical form taken
by a god when he intercedes
periodically to save the world from
peril, usually referring to Vishnu's
many incarnations.

ayudha puja
worship of weapons as
embodiments of an aspect of the
god with whom they are associated.

Bhadrakali
probably a nature goddess adapted
by Shaivas into a sometimes wrathful
form of Durga who bestows boons
on children in return for sacrifice.

bhakti
intense, uncompromising devotion
to a personal god, aspiring to
mystical union with the divine.

Bhikshatana
'Lord as Beggar' – Shiva taking
the form of a wandering ascetic
in atonement for cutting off one
of god Brahma's five heads.

Bhu
earth.

Bhu Devi
Earth Goddess, personification
of the earth and one of two
consorts of Vishnu.

Brahman
highest caste in India, generally
synonymous with priestly class,
entitled to perform Hindu rites
and sacrifices; authors of the
Brahmanas, designed to
guide Brahmans in hymns and
performance of various rituals.

Chandesha
Shaivite poet-saint, originally
a young cowherd whose faith
was rewarded by granting of
grace and appointment as the
earthly head of Shiva's *ganas*.

Chandrashekhara
'Lord Crowned with the Moon' –
benign form of Shiva, smiling and
with crescent moon prominently
displayed in his hair.

channavira
jewelled ornament worn as
neckpiece, falling between
the breasts and secured behind
the waist.

chit sabha
gold-roofed hall housing cult image
of Shiva Nataraja at Nataraja temple,
Chidambaram.

cire perdue
'lost wax' metal-casting technique
whereby wax model is enclosed
in clay mould, melted out through
vents and replaced by molten
metal (usually bronze).

damaru
small, double-ended, hourglass-
shaped drum held by Shiva, its sound
denoting the primordial creation
and destruction of the universe.

dana
gift or charitable donation, especially
in religious context.

darshan
'seeing [god]' – auspicious viewing
of deity's cult image, conferring
blessings on the devotee.

Devi
goddess who is worshipped in many
forms, but principally associated with
Shiva as Durga or Bhadrakali.

dharma
established belief and practice,
law or doctrine.

Dravidian
peoples of south India.

Durga
'Impassable One' – destroyer
of demon forces; composite of
many local deities who assumed
prominence as war-like expression
of Uma-Parvati's personality.

ganas
mischievous dwarf-like figures
derived from nature spirits (*yaksha*
and *yakshi*) and adopted into
Hinduism as Shiva's faithful
attendants, led by Ganesha.

Ganesha
'Lord of the Ganas' – elephant-
headed son of Shiva and Parvati,
venerated as remover of obstacles
and god of wisdom; lord of the
ganas.

garbhagrha
'womb chamber' – sanctum
of Hindu temple, where cult
image is housed.

Garuda
mythical eagle, typically represented
as half-bird, half-human, who serves
as Vishnu's mount (*vahana*).

gopis and *gopas*
cowherd women and men.

Hanuman
monkey chief and ally of Rama,
son of wind god Vayu, and subject
of cult following for his martial
prowess and loyal friendship.

iconometry
rules determining proportions
of images and buildings.

jata
knot of matted hair, especially
of Shiva; hallmark of Shiva's
followers (*risis*).

Kaliya
five-headed demon-snake who
terrorised villagers along River
Yamuna (Jumna) but was subdued
by Krishna.

Karaikkal Ammaiyar
sixth-century female devotee
of Shiva, included in canon of poet-
saints; famed for renouncing bodily
beauty to serve Shiva better.

karana
classified and codified dance
movements.

Krishna
worshipped as avatar of Vishnu, especially at his birth place near Mathura, originating as local pastoral deity and identified as hero of *Mahabharata* epic and expounder of *Bhagavad Gita*.

Laskshmana
younger brother of Rama.

Lakshmi
goddess of motherhood and fertility; regarded in early times as personification of the earth (Bhu Lakshmi) and later as goddess of fortune, riches and beauty, consort of Vishnu.

lalitasana
relaxed sitting posture with one leg pendant, the other bent at the knee.

linga
aniconic pillar-like symbol of Shiva, typically in phallic form evoking Shiva's progenitive powers; fertility symbol, especially connected with Shiva as Bijavin (Giver of Seed).

makara
mythical sea creature combining elements of fish, crocodile, lion and elephant, symbolising life-giving power of the waters.

Manikkavachakar
ninth-century Shaivite poet-saint; one of the *nalvar* ('Revered Four').

Mushalagan
dwarf-like figure signifying ignorance and darkness, upon whom Shiva as Nataraja dances in conquest; Tamil version of Sanskrit term 'Apasamara'.

muvar
'Revered Three' Shaivite poet-saints – child saint Sambandar, Appar and Sundarar.

nalvar
'Revered Four' Shaivite poet-saints – the *muvar* and Manikkavachakar.

Nandi
'joyful' – calf-bull associated with Shiva from earliest period, when he was probably also understood as a form of Shiva; later seen as Shiva's mount but still worshipped in own right.

Narasimha
'Man-lion' – fourth appearance of Vishnu in wrathful half-man, half-lion form, to overcome tyranny of the demon ruler Hiranyakashipu.

Nataraja
'Lord of Dance' – Shiva as cosmological dancer, typically represented in *ananda tandava* posture; particularly associated with Chidambaram temple.

nayanmar
'leaders' – revered Shaivite *bhakta* saints remembered for their absolute devotion and some especially for their poetry and songs of praise.

Parameshvari
an aspect of Devi as Uma-Parvati.

Parvati
wife of Shiva, connected with mountain tribes of Himalayas; referred to as Uma in south India, where she is said to be sister of Vishnu; gracious, friendly and maternal fertility deity.

patal perra talam
'place sung by the saints' – temple or holy place celebrated in hymn by poet-saints.

prabha
decorative circle of flames framing sculptural image of deity.

prasada
flowers or food offered to deity in Hindu ritual and then distributed to devotees as act of grace by god.

puja
ritual acts to invoke and honour a deity, performed by presiding Brahman priests at temples, by village priests at local shrines, or by householders at household shrines.

punya
religious merit.

Rama
seventh avatar of Vishnu, who appeared as king of Ayodhya to counter threat to world order posed by demon Ravana, as recounted in the *Ramayana* epic.

ratha
temple chariot designed to transport processional images of deities during temple festival processions.

Ravana
ten-headed demon king of Lanka (Sri Lanka) and Rama's main adversary in the *Ramayana*.

Rukmini
'wearer of golden ornaments' – Krishna's senior queen, daughter of king of Kundinapura.

sacred thread
cord worn by high-caste Brahmans, the 'twice-born'.

Sambandar
prominent Shaiva poet-saint, believed to have lived in seventh century; usually portrayed as a dancing child.

Shaivite
pertaining to Shiva.

Shiva
'Auspicious One' – complex, many-faceted deity, creator and destroyer, both auspicious and dangerous; along with Vishnu and Devi, principal cult deity of Hindu India.

Shrikantha
'Lord of the Auspicious Neck' – Shiva as drinker of poison from the primordial ocean that threatened to destroy the universe.

shrivatsa
triangular or rhomboid chest mark, attribute of Vishnu.

silpasastras
texts providing technical and aesthetic guidance to those empowered to make arts and crafts.

Sita
wife of Rama and heroine of the *Ramayana* epic.

Somaskanda
Shiva shown in family ensemble of Uma-Parvati and their child Skanda; especially popular in south India in the Pallava (c. 600–850/900) and Chola (c. 950–1250) periods.

sthapati
artisans, architects, artists, metal sculptors, makers of icons.

Sundarar
ninth-century Shaivite poet-saint; one of the *muvar* ('Revered Three').

Telegu
Dravidian language spoken in Andhra Pradesh and neighbouring regions.

Tevaram
corpus of devotional poems composed by Shaiva poet-saints.

tilaka
sectarian mark worn on forehead by Hindus to denote religious allegiance; believed to have talismanic properties.

tirtha
holy place of pilgrimage, associated with rivers and bathing places because water is believed to wash away sins.

tribhanga
'triple bend' posture.

Tripuravijaya
'Victor of the Three Cities' – Shiva as destroyer of three powerful demons and their three cities, shown with the arrow that he used to slay them.

ula
Tamil word referring to both a procession and a poem describing a procession.

Uma
mother aspect of Parvati and preferred term for this goddess in south India.

utsavamurti
'festival images' – movable images of gods and saints, generally bronze, paraded during temple festivals.

utsavas
religious festivals focused on processions and held periodically, the most spectacular being annual parades.

vahana
animal mount of deity.

Vaishnava
pertaining to Vishnu.

Varaha
third avatar of Vishnu as giant boar who rescued the Earth Goddess from waters of the cosmic ocean; also known as Bhu Varaha.

Vedas
'knowledge' – sacred Hindu scriptures, regarded by orthodoxy as divine revelation, comprising the four *Vedas* (hymns), *Brahmanas* (priestly treatises), *Aranyakas* (esoteric texts) and *Upanishads* (philosophical and mystical treatises).

veshti
male skirt, also known as *dhoti* or *lungi*.

vihara
Buddhist monastery; in India, especially associated with rock-cut halls.

vimana
'chariot of the gods' – main tower of temple, considered to be a divine aerial palace inhabited by the gods; also applied to temple as a whole.

vina
long-necked stringed instrument with globular resonator.

Vinadhara
'Player of the Vina' – Shiva represented holding a *vina*, denoting his role as divine teacher of music.

Vishnu
major Hindu god with many avatars, his principal forms being Matsya, Kurma, Varaha, Narasimha, Vamana, Parashurama, Rama, Krishna, Buddha and Kalki.

visarjana
ritual performed by priest at end of worship (*puja*) to send away the deity after temporary inhabitation of icon.

Vrishbhavana
Shiva as 'Rider of the Bull' shown with his mount, Nandi, sometimes accompanied by Uma-Parvati.

vyakhyana
hand gesture of explanation, especially associated with Shiva and his followers.

Yama
god of death.

Selected Bibliography

Aiyer 1934
K.V. Subrahmanya Aiyer,
'The Smaller Leiden Plates of
Kulottunga I', *Epigraphia Indica*,
22 (1933–34)

Ali 2004
D. Ali, *Courtly Culture and Political
Life in Early Medieval India*,
New York, 2004

Aravamuthan 1931
T.G. Aravamuthan, *Portrait Sculpture
in South India*, London, 1931

Balasubrahmanyam 1971
S.R. Balasubrahmanyam, *Early Chola
Temples: Parantaka I to Rajaraja I,
AD 907–985*, Delhi, 1971

Barrett 1965
D. Barrett, *Early Cola Bronzes*, Bombay,
Bhulabhai Memorial Institute, 1965

Barrett 1974
D. Barrett, *Early Cola Architecture
and Sculpture, 866–1014 AD*,
London, 1974

Basak 1936
R.G. Basak, 'The Puri Plates of
Madhavavarman-Sainyabhita',
Epigraphia Indica, 23 (1935–36)

Carman and Narayanan 1989
J. Carman and V. Narayanan,
*The Tamil Veda: Pillan's Interpretation
of the Tiruvaymoli*, Chicago and
London, 1989

Catlin 1991
A. Catlin, '"Vatapi Ganapatim":
Sculptural, Poetic, and Musical Texts
in a Hymn to Ganesa', in *Ganesh:
Studies of an Asian God*,
R.L. Brown (ed.), Albany, 1991

Coburn 1991
T. Coburn, *Encountering the Goddess*,
Albany, 1991

Cort 2001
J.E. Cort, *Jains in the World: Religious
Values and Ideology in India*,
Oxford and New York, 2001

Davis 1991
R.H. Davis, *Ritual in an Oscillating
Universe*, Princeton, 1991

Davis 1997
R.H. Davis, *Lives of Indian Images*,
Princeton, 1997

Davis 1998
R.H. Davis, 'The Story of the
Disappearing Jains: Retelling the
Saiva-Jain Encounter in Medieval
South India', in *Open Boundaries:
Jain Communities and Cultures
in Indian History*, J.E. Cort (ed.),
Albany, 1998

Dehejia 1988
V. Dehejia, *Slaves of the Lord: The Path
of the Tamil Saints*, Delhi, 1988

Dehejia 1990A
V. Dehejia, *Art of the Imperial Cholas*,
New York, 1990

Dehejia 1990B
V. Dehejia, *Antal and the Path
of Love*, New York, 1990

Dehejia 1995
V. Dehejia, 'Iconographic Transference
between Krsna and Three Saiva
Saints', in *Indian Art and
Connoisseurship: Essays in Honour
of Douglas Barrett*, J. Guy (ed.),
New Delhi, 1995, pp. 140–9

Dehejia 1999
V. Dehejia, 'Poetic Visions of
the Great Goddess: Tamil Nadu',
in *Devi, The Great Goddess: Female
Divinity in South Asian Art*, exh. cat.,
Smithsonian Institution, Washington,
D.C., 1999, p. 10

Delhi 1962
Cire Perdue Casting in India, R. Reeves,
exh. cat., Crafts Museum, Delhi, 1962

Eck 1981
D.L. Eck, *Darsan: Seeing the Divine
Image in India*, Chambersburg, 1981

Eck 1998
D.L. Eck, *Darsan: Seeing the
Divine Image in India*, 3rd ed.,
New York, 1998

Elliot 1877
H.M. Elliot, *The History of India
as Told by its own Historians*, 3 vols,
ed. J. Dowson, 1867–77

Gangoly 1915
O.C. Gangoly, *South Indian Bronzes*,
London, 1915

Gravely and Ramachandran 1932
F.H. Gravely and T.N. Ramachandran,
*Catalogue of South Indian Hindu
Metal Images in the Madras Museum*,
Madras, 1932

Grunfeld 1988
F.V. Grunfeld, *Rodin: A Biography*,
London, 1988

Guy 1994
J. Guy, 'The Lost Temples of
Nagapattinam and Quanzhou:
A Study in Sino-Indian Relations',
Silk Road Art and Archaeology, 3
(1993–94), pp. 291–310

Guy 1995
J. Guy (ed.), *Indian Art and
Connisseurship: Essays in Honour
of Douglas Barrett*, New Delhi, 1995

Guy 1997
J. Guy, 'Indian Dance in the Temple
Context', in *Dancing to the Flute:
Music and Dance in Indian Art*,
J. Masselos, et al. (eds) exh. cat., Art
Gallery of New South Wales, Sydney,
1997, pp. 26–36

Guy 2001
J. Guy, 'Tamil Merchant Guilds and the
Quanzhou Trade', in *The Emporium
of the World: Maritime Quanzhou
1000–1400*, A. Schottenhamer (ed.),
Leiden, 2001, pp. 283–308

Guy 2004
J. Guy, 'The Nataraja Murti and Chidambaram: Genesis of a Cult Image', in *Chidambaram: Home of Nataraja*, V. Nanda and G. Michell (eds), Mumbai, 2004, pp. 70–81

Guy 2005
J. Guy, 'Southern Buddhism – Traces and Transmissions', in *Proceedings of the 16th European Association of South Asian Archaeology Conference, College de France, Paris, 2001*, C. Jarrige and V. Lefevre (eds), Paris, 2005, pp. 495–504

Heifitz 1985
H. Heifitz, *The Origin of the Young God: Kalidasa's Kumarasambhava*, Berkeley, 1985

Hopkins 2002
S. P. Hopkins, *Singing the Body of God: The Hymns of Vedantadesika in their South Indian Tradition*, Oxford, 2002

Ingalls 1965
D. H. H. Ingalls (trans.), *Sanskrit Poetry from Vidyakara's 'Treasury'*, Cambridge, 1965

Iyer and Gros 1985
T. V. Gopal Iyer and F. Gros (eds), *Tevaram. Hymnes Sivaites du pays Tamoul*, Pondicherry, 1985

Johnson 1972
B. Johnson, 'An Examination and Treatment Report', in *Krishna: The Cowherd King*, P. Pal (ed.), Los Angeles County Museum of Art, Los Angeles, 1972

Kannan 2003
R. Kannan, *Manual on the Bronzes in the Government Museum, Chennai*, Chennai, 2003

Keilhorn 1888
F. Keilhorn, 'Mau Chandella Inscription of Madanavarman', *Epigraphia Indica*, 1 (1888)

Lefeber 2005
R. Lefeber, *Ramayana Book Four: Kishkindha. By Valmiki*, New York, 2005

Luders 1901
H. Luders, 'Two Pillar Inscriptions of the Time of Krishnaraya of Vijayanagara', *Epigraphia Indica*, 6 (1900–01)

Mer 1912
Madras Epigraphy Report, Madras, 1912

Miller 1986
B. Stoler Miller (trans.), *The Bhagavad-Gita: Krishna's Counsel in Time of War*, New York, 1986

Mirashi 1942
V. V. Mirashi, 'Ratanpur Stone Inscription of the Kalachuri Year 915', *Epigraphia Indica*, 26 (1941–42)

Nagaswamy 1960
R. Nagaswamy, 'New Bronze Finds from Tiruvenkadu', *Transactions of the Archaeological Society of South India, 1959–1960*, pp. 108–22

Nagaswamy 1961
R. Nagaswamy, 'Rare Bronzes from Kongu County', *Lalit Kala*, 9–10 (1961), pp. 34–40

Nagaswamy 1967
R. Nagaswamy, 'Kongu Bronzes in the Victoria and Albert Museum', *Lalit Kala*, 13 (1967), pp. 41–5

Nagaswamy 1979A
R. Nagaswamy, 'A Nataraja and an Inscribed Uma from Karaiviram Village', *Lalit Kala*, 19 (1979), pp. 17–19

Nagaswamy 1979B
R. Nagaswamy, 'Chidambaram Bronzes', *Lalit Kala*, 19 (1979), pp. 9–16 and plates

Nagaswamy 1987
R. Nagaswamy, 'Archaeological Finds in South India: Esalam Bronzes and Copperplates', *Bulletin de l'Ecole Francaise de l'Extreme-Orient*, 76 (1987), pp. 1–68

Nagaswamy 1995
R. Nagaswamy, 'On Dating South Indian Bronzes', in *Indian Art and Connoisseurship: Essays in Honour of Douglas Barrett*, J. Guy (ed.), New Delhi, 1995, pp. 101–29

Nagaswamy 2005
R. Nagaswamy, 'Tripurantaka, Vinadhara Dakshinamurti, or Kiratamurti?', in *Aspects of Art and Architecture of South India*, R. Nagaswamy (ed.), New Delhi, 2005

Narayanan 1985
V. Narayanan, 'Arcavatara: On Earth as He is in Heaven', in *Gods of Flesh, Gods of Stone: The Embodiment of the Divinity in India*, J. Waghorne and N. Cutler (eds), Chambersburg, 1985

Narayanan 1994
V. Narayanan, *The Vernacular Veda: Revelation, Recitation, and Ritual*, Columbia, 1994

Nead 1992
L. Nead, *The Female Nude: Art, Obscenity and Sexuality*, London and New York, 1992

New Delhi 1983
Masterpieces of Early South Indian Bronzes, R. Nagaswamy, exh. cat., National Museum, New Delhi, 1983

Orr 2004
L. C. Orr, 'Processions in the Medieval South Indian Temple: Sociology, Sovereignty and Soteriology', in *South-Indian Horizons: Felicitation Volume for Francois Gros*, J-L. Chevillard (ed.), Pondicherry, 2004, pp. 437–70.

Pal 1972
P. Pal (ed.), *Krishna: The Cowherd King*, Los Angeles, 1972

Peterson 1989
I. V. Peterson, *Poems to Siva: The Hymns of the Tamil Saints*, Princeton, 1989

Peterson 1998
I. V. Peterson, 'Sramanas against the Tamil Way: Jains as Others in Tamil Saiva Literature', in *Open Boundaries: Jain Communities and Cultures in Indian History*, J. E. Cort (ed.), Albany, 1998

Pollock 2005
S. L. Pollock (trans.), *Ramayana Book Two: Ayodhya by Valmiki*, New York, 2005

Pope 1900
G. U. Pope (trans.), *Tiruvacagam*, Oxford, 1900

Prasad 1990
P. Prasad, *Sanskrit Inscriptions of the Delhi Sultanate 1191–1526*, Delhi, 1990

Ramachandran 1954
T. N. Ramachandran, 'The Nagapattinam and other Buddhist Bronzes in the Madras Museum', *Bulletin of the Madras Museum*, n.s. VII, 1 (1954)

Ramachandran 1956
T. N. Ramachandran, 'Bronze Images from Tirunvenkadu-Svetaranya (Tanjore District)', *Lalit Kala*, 3 (1956), pp. 55–62

Ramanujan 1973
A. K. Ramanujan (trans.), *Speaking of Siva*, New Delhi, 1973

Ramanujan 1993
A. K. Ramanujan (trans.), *Hymns for the Drowning: Poems for Visnu by Nammalvar*, New Delhi, 1993

Rathnasabapathy 1982
S. Rathnasabapathy, *The Thanjavur Art Gallery Bronze Sculptures*, Tanjavur, Tanjavur Art Gallery Administration, 1982

Rodin 1921
A. Rodin, A. Coomaraswamy, E.-B. Havell and V. Goloubew, *Ars Asiatica, vol. III: Sculptures Civaites*, Brussels and Paris, 1921

Sastri 1955
N. K. A. Sastri, *The Colas*, Madras, 1955

Shulman 1990
D. D. Shulman, *Songs of the Harsh Devotee: The Tevaram of Cuntaramurttinayanar*, Philadelphia, 1990

SII 1916
E. Hultzsch and V. Venkayya (eds), *South Indian Inscriptions II*, Delhi, 1916

SII 1929
E. Hultzsch and V. Venkayya (eds), *South Indian Inscriptions III*, Delhi, 1929

Sivaramamurti 1974
C. Sivaramamurti, *Nataraja in Art, Thought, and Literature*, New Delhi, 1974

Smith 1996
David Smith, *Dance of Siva: Religion, Art, and Poetry in South India*, Cambridge, 1996

Soifer 1991
D. A. Soifer, *The Myths of Narasimha and Vamana: Two Avatars in Cosmological Perspective*, Albany, 1991

Srinivasan 1963
P. R. Srinivasan, *Bronzes of South India*, Madras, Government Museum, 1963

Stein 1978
B. Stein (ed.), *South Indian Temples: An Analytical Reconsideration*, Delhi, 1978

Subramaniam 1977
V. K. Subramaniam, *Saundaryalahiri*, Delhi, 1977

Takakusu 1896
J. Takakusu (trans.), *I-tsing. A Record of the Buddhist Religion as Practised in India and the Malay Archipelago AD 671–695*, London, 1896

Vedachalam 1999
V. Vedachalam, 'Pandiya nattil Natarajisvaram', in *Tolliyal Nokkil Tamilaham*, Chennai, 1999

Venkataraman 1976
B. Venkataraman, *Temple Art Under the Chola Queens*, Faridabad, 1976

Venkataraman 1985
B. Venkataraman, *Rajaraesvaram: The Pinnacle of Chola Art*, Madras, 1985

Washington 2003
The Sensuous and the Sacred: Chola Bronzes from South India, Vidya Dehejia, exh. cat., Smithsonian Institution, Washington, D.C., 2002–03

Wentworth
B. Wentworth, 'Women's Bodies, Earthly Kingdom: Mapping the Presence of God in the *Tirukkailaya Nana Ula*' (Ph.D. diss., Divinity School, University of Chicago)

Yocum 1982
G. Yocum, *Hymns to the Dancing Siva*, New Delhi, 1982

Yule and Burnell 1886
H. Yule and A. C. Burnell, *Hobson-Jobson: Glossary of Anglo-Indian Colloquial Words and Phrases*, London, 1886

List of Works

1
Shiva as Nataraja (Lord of Dance)
Eleventh century
Bronze, 111.5 × 101.65 cm
The Cleveland Museum of Art,
Purchase from the J. H. Wade Fund, 1930.331

2
Shiva as Nataraja (Lord of Dance)
c.1100
Bronze, 86 × 107 cm
Government Museum, Chennai

3
**Shiva as Tripuravijaya
(Victor of the Three Cities)
and Consort**
c.950–60
Bronze, 81.9 × 48.7 cm
and 65.1 × 16.5 cm
The Cleveland Museum of Art,
John L. Severance Fund, 1961.94

4
**Shiva as Tripuravijaya
(Victor of the Three Cities)**
c.970
Bronze, 97.2 × 37.5 cm
National Museum, New Delhi

5
**Shiva as Chandrashekhara
(Lord Crowned with the Moon)**
c.990
Bronze, H. 51 cm
The British Museum, London

6
**Shiva as Shrikantha
(Lord of the Auspicious Neck)**
c.970
Bronze, H. 58.4 cm
The British Museum, London

7
**Shiva as Vinadhara
(Player of the Vina)**
c.1000
Bronze, H. 76.1 cm
The Cleveland Museum of Art,
Leonard C.Hanna, Jr., Fund, 1971.117

8
Nandi
c.1200
Bronze, H. 51.4 cm
Asia Society, New York, Collection of
Mr and Mrs John D. Rockefeller 3rd, 1979.30

9
**Shiva as Somaskanda
(with Uma and Skanda)**
c.1100
Bronze, 70 × 97 cm
Henry Cornell

10
**Devi Uma Parameshvari
(Great Goddess Uma)**
c.1012
Bronze, H. 88.9 cm
Asia Society, New York, Collection of
Mr and Mrs John D. Rockefeller 3rd, 1979.19

11
Durga
c.970
Bronze, 57.2 × 20 cm
Brooklyn Museum, New York, Gift of Georgia
and Michael de Havenon in memory of
William H.Wolff, 1992.142

12
Bhadrakali
c.1250
Bronze, 75.4 × 30.5 cm
National Museum, New Delhi

13
**Trident with Shiva as
Vrishabhavana (Rider of the Bull)**
c.950
Bronze, H. 83.6 cm
The British Museum, London

14
Ganesha
c.1070
Bronze, H. 50.2 cm
The Cleveland Museum of Art, Gift of Katharine
Holden Thayer, 1970.62

15
Saint Sambandar
c.1050–75
Bronze, H. 60 cm
Dr Siddharth Bhansali, New Orleans

16
Saint Sambandar
c.1250
Bronze, 42 × 22 cm
Linden-Museum, Stuttgart

17
Saint Karaikkal Ammaiyar
Twelfth century
Copper alloy, 23.2 × 16.5 cm
The Metropolitan Museum of Art, New York,
Purchase, Edward J. Gallagher, Jr., Bequest, in
memory of his father, Edward Joseph Gallagher,
his mother, Ann Hay Gallagher, and his son,
Edward Joseph Gallagher III, 1982 (1982.220.11)

18
Saint Manikkavachakar
c.1100
Bronze, 50.2 × 21.8 cm
National Museum, New Delhi

19
Saint Chandesha
c.970
Bronze, H. 48 cm
The British Museum, London

20
Vishnu
c.1100
Bronze, 84.7 × 35.6 cm
The National Museum, New Delhi

21
**Bhu Varaha Embracing Goddess
Earth**
Thirteenth century
Bronze, 45.5 × 30 cm
Victoria and Albert Museum, London

22
Yoga Narasimha
c.1250
Bronze, H. 55.2 cm
The Cleveland Museum of Art,
Gift of Dr Norman Zaworski, 1973.187

23
Sita
c.980–90
Bronze, 66 × 20 cm
Linden-Museum, Stuttgart

24
Monkey General Hanuman
c.1020
Bronze, H. 41 cm
Victoria and Albert Museum, London,
Bequest of Lord Curzon

25
Krishna Dancing on Kaliya
Eleventh century
Bronze, H. 87.6 cm
Asia Society, New York, Collection of Mr
and Mrs John D. Rockefeller 3rd, 1979.22

26
**Krishna, with Consorts
Rukmini and Satyabhama
and Divine Eagle Garuda**
Thirteenth century
Bronze, 68.9 × 24.8 cm, 87 × 40.6 cm,
71.8 × 23.5 cm, 49.8 × 22.9 cm
Los Angeles County Museum of Art,
Gift of Mr and Mrs Hal B. Wallis

27
Krishna Rajamannar
Twelfth century
Bronze, H. 101.5 cm
Mr D. A. Latchford Collection

28
Jina, probably Mahavira
Tenth century
Bronze, 74.3 × 35.6 cm
Private collection

Lenders to the Exhibition

Dr Siddharth Bhansali

Chennai
Government Museum

Cleveland
The Cleveland Museum of Art

Henry Cornell

Mr D. A. Latchford

London
The British Museum
Victoria and Albert Museum

Los Angeles
Los Angeles County Museum
   of Art

New Delhi
National Museum

New York
Asia Society, Rockefeller
   Collection
Brooklyn Museum
The Metropolitan Museum
   of Art

Stuttgart
Linden-Museum

*and others who wish
to remain anonymous*

Photographic Acknowledgements

Index

All references are to page numbers.
Those in **bold** type indicate
catalogue plates, and those in
italic type indicate essay illustrations.

Benefactors of the Royal Academy of Arts